Roots
of Delinquency

INFANCY, ADOLESCENCE AND CRIME

Michael Wadsworth

BOOKS
10 East 53d St., New York 10022
(a division of Harper & Row Publishers, Inc.)

First published in 1979 by Martin Robertson & Company Limited., 108 Cowley Road, Oxford OX4 1JF. Published in the USA 1979 by Harper & Row Publishers Inc., Barnes & Noble Import Division.

ISBN 0-06-497305-0

Typeset by Pioneer Ltd., East Sussex
Printed and bound in Britain by Richard Clay Ltd.
at The Chaucer Press, Bungay, Suffolk.

Contents

Preface

In Tom Stoppard's *Jumpers* George Moore, a professor of philosophy, remarks that experience has taught him 'that to attempt to sustain the attention of rival schools of academics by argument alone is tantamount to constructing a gothic arch out of junket'. Anyone who has tried to review and to reconcile the various theories that have set out to account for crime and delinquency will know that to attempt to fit them together in a coherent and constructive way is a comparable task. Whilst making no claim to such an achievement, because of the nature and wide range of the information I have been fortunate enough to work with, I have been obliged in the course of this work to consider a large number of theories from several disciplines. And although I have scarcely begun to construct an arch across theories and across disciplines, the experience of this work has convinced me of the necessity for an arch. I hope that I shall be able to convince others of this necessity and perhaps have provided some suggestions about how we might begin its construction.

The information I have used is all part of the National Survey of Health and Development, which is a longitudinal study that has regularly investigated the health, growth and development of 5362 children from their birth in March 1946 to the present day. The study was initiated by a joint committee of the Royal College of Obstetricians and Gynaecologists, the Institute of Child Health and the Society of Medical Officers of Health — the Population Investigation Committee. Were it not for the enthusiasm and persistence of the National Survey's director, Dr J.W.B. Douglas, it would have perished many years ago, as indeed it might have done without the continuing help and interest of the Population Investigation Committee, under its chairman Professor D.V. Glass. The National Survey has continued for thirty years primarily because of the continuing interest and cooperation of both the men and women who are its subjects, and their parents. Without the generous help of education officers, medical officers of health, teachers, school doctors, school nurses and youth employment officers throughout the country this mass of detailed information could not have been collected. The National Survey is now supported by the Medical Research Council but has also received support from the Nuffield Foundation, the Ford Foundation, the Population Council and various government departments, and it is particularly appropriate to acknowledge the assistance and encouragement of the Home Office Research Unit, the Criminal Record Office at New Scotland Yard, the Home Office Statistical Department, the Probation Service and the Child Care Service.

Many people have influenced my thinking about this investigation. It is particularly necessary to thank my director Dr J.W.B. Douglas and my erstwhile tutor Professor T.P. Morris (some part of this work was presented as a doctoral thesis), as well as Professor F.M. McClintock. I have been much helped by my colleagues in this MRC Unit, especially Elizabeth Atkins and Janet Tillott, and by Susannah Brown and Margaret Hall at the London School of Economics. I am also grateful to the various colleagues, both in the University of London and in other universities, who have given me the opportunity to 'try out' my ideas on their staff and students, and also to various friends, especially Ann Cartwright and Brigid Davies, who have commented on the manuscript — what Hexter calls 'confidential banana-peel slipping. It consists in getting a friendly, skilled, but critical reader to go over one's work before one presents it in public.' To all of these, and particularly to my family, Jane, Emma and Harry, for their patience and interest, I offer warm thanks.

Michael Wadsworth

Foreword

The quest for understanding has led to a plethora of theories regarding physical, psychological, and sociological conditions conducive to criminal behavior. Many of these theories have been examined through cross-sectional comparisons or by use of retrospective techniques. Neither approach, however, is adequate to the task. Cross-sectional comparisons may show differences which were not present prior to criminal behavior or, conversely, may fail to show important differentiating conditions which would have been detected had comparisons been made at a prior time. When comparisons include information about the past, the information is suspect because differences may be due to reporting biases systematically related to the criminal and the non-criminal dimensions being studied.

If the two groups were equally successful prior to the time when delinquency began, for example, studies which show that a criminal population is less successful in school than a non-criminal population would be wrongly interpreted as indicating that a lack of success in school tends to lead to delinquency. If low pulse rates differentiate those who will become delinquent from their peers and this difference disappears, studies which compare people who have become delinquents with those who have not and find no differences could be missing an important clue to the etiology of delinquency. If delinquents tend to minimize self-criticism, studies which show no differences between delinquents and nondelinquents in their retrospective reports of pre-adolescent deceptions may mask real differences which could be helpful for understanding patterns of deviant behavior.

Whether considered as a procedure for discovering laws of development, bases for valid predictions, or causally relevant conditions, information about concurrent events gathered over a period of many years is fundamental to the understanding of crime.

In writing *Roots of Delinquency,* Michael Wadsworth has used an exceptionally rich collection of information about the lives of men and women born in England and Wales during March, 1946. Data for his study include information gathered annually or biannually from 1946 to 1961, with criminal convictions to the age of twenty-one as the dependent variable.

Wadsworth classifies the subjects in terms of the "social accept-ability" of their most serious crimes. He shows that those who have committed the "least acceptable" offenses are most clearly differen-tiated from nondelinquents.

The book contains a wealth of information about conditions which distinguish predelinquents from nondelinquents. Predelinquents, for example, relatively more frequently had experienced parental loss; teachers had considered the mothers of predelinquents to be disinterested in their children's school activities; the children later to become delinquent had lower pulse rates than did their classmates; secondary school teachers had rated a higher proportion of pre-delinquents as resentful of criticism, aggressive, and prepared to lie. Knowledge of these conditions helps to establish a sequential ordering of events. The use of multiple regression procedures and discriminant function analyses help to place these events in proper perspective.

I suspect that this book will give rise to some healthy and fruitful controversies among those interested in understanding criminal behavior. Dr. Wadsworth gives primacy to such descriptors as family size and structure and to social class. He suggests that the variables based upon assessments by home visitors and by teachers reflect common stereotypes. These interpretations deserve consideration.

Alternative interpretations, however, are equally plausible. Home visitors may have been correct in their judgments that homes already severed when the target child was four were providing poorer care than homes not-yet or never-to-be severed. Teachers, too, may have given reasonably valid measures of the mother's interest in school; these ratings were related to (independent) measures of absence from school due to accidental injury. If accidental injuries occur more frequently in the absence of supervision by the mother, the latter relationship supports the validity of the interest measure. Both the home visitors and the teachers provided information which could be interpreted as showing that poor maternal care is a precursor of criminal behavior. If these are unreliable measures, the strength of their relationship to subsequent behavior would, of course, be diminished.

My own research suggests that maternal attitudes and family conflict may be fundamental to understanding subsequent development of criminal behavior. Family size and structure as well as social class might be related to criminality as indicators are to the events which they signal. Perhaps neither broken homes nor family size yield an account of the variance in crime rates beyond what they reveal about family affect and interaction.

One can anticipate further important studies developing from the questions to which this book gives rise. By presenting longitudinal evidence about the development of crime, *Roots of Delinquency* should be a lasting contribution to the field of criminology.

Drexel University
Philadelphia

Joan McCord
Professor of Sociology

CHAPTER 1

Introduction

There is considerable public awareness of and alarm at apparent rises in the amount of crime. In their review of trends McClintock and Avison (1968) observed that

> ... the number of crimes recorded by the police increased from 438,085 in 1955 to 1,133,882 in 1965. This represents an overall increase of 159% and an annual gross rate of approximately 10%. During these recent eleven years there has, of course, been a substantial increase in the population of England and Wales, but even when the annual volume of crime is related to the size of the population, the upward trend is still marked. ... The actual incidence of crime per 100,000 of the population increased from 986 in 1955 to 2,374 in 1965. This somewhat more refined assessment still gives an increase of 141% for the eleven year period. [p. 33]

Debate continues as to how far such apparent increases are the result of greater public willingness to report crime and greater police willingness to prosecute, but it is indisputable that expenditure on crime is rising. McClintock and Avison (1968) showed that during the years 1954 to 1965 not only did the total number of larcenies and break-in offences more than double, but also the estimated average value of property stolen per theft (excluding robbery) almost doubled and the estimated overall value of property stolen rose by a factor of five. The most recent (1974) published official statistics of the value of property stolen (that is to say, reported offences of burglary, theft and robbery) have been used to estimate that its value was in excess of forty-four million pounds. The cost of services associated with crime has also risen. Martin and Wilson (1969) noted that between 1950 and 1965 the cost of the police, at 1969 prices, rose by 200 per cent and that

> ... during the fifteen years from 1950 to 1965 the police share of gross national expenditure, although subject to fluctuations, increased substantially. Gross national expenditure rose by 163%, public spending (excluding defence) by 202% and the cost of the police service by 256%.

1

Over the same fifteen years the actual strength of the police service (excluding civilians) rose from 62,910 to 84,430. [p. 248]

More recently Borrell and Cashinella (1975) observed that

... it has often been argued by leading economists that theft, when taken totally as a loss to the community, the costs of insuring against it, the cost of police investigation, the employment of security services in attempts to stop it, probably costs Britain as much as 2% of its national income at around 850 million pounds a year. [p. 113]

In short, they find that 'crime costs Britain's taxpayers more than 500 million pounds a year and yet seven out of ten of all crimes committed remain unsolved' (p. 120).

Sociologists and psychologists have for many years looked at differences between offenders and non-offenders in a search for explanations of why offending occurred. The explanations and descriptions of contributing factors have ranged across a wide spectrum, from genetic predisposition and various concepts of innate criminality, to factors in personal life such as broken homes, physical characteristics such as height and shape, and such social factors as social mobility and social environment, and the capitalist structure and functions of Western society. Psychological studies of the committal of crime continue to be concerned with individual pathology, faulty conditioning, personality differences, uncontrollable *id* forces and so on, accepting crimes as given events to be explained and understood. Sociological studies, on the other hand, question the fact that some acts are identified as crimes whilst others are not, and are interested both in how certain behaviour comes to be defined as crime and in the social context of crime at both the macro and the micro levels.

At the micro level much attention has been devoted to the immediate social context of crimes. Matza (1969) and Box (1971), for example, have both paid close attention to the *processes* of the identification of suspects, of arrests, of charges being made, of plea bargaining and of sentencing. From this work and its concern with the inequalities of the situation where some offenders could avoid official classification as criminals and some could not, there naturally followed a number of self-report studies of criminal behaviour. These endeavoured to show that crime is committed by a very wide range of people, a range that cuts across the apparent social-class, ethnic, economic and other social differences in incidence of officially defined crime that some criminologists have sought to explain.

At the macro social level sociologists began, as Matza (1964) noted,

> ... with the observation that there are gross differences in the rate of delinquency by class, by ethnic affiliation, by urban or rural residence, by region and perhaps by nation and historical epoch. From these gross differences the sociologist infers that something beyond the intimacy of family surroundings is operative in the emergence of delinquency patterns; something in the cultural and social atmosphere apparent in sections of society. [p. 17]

New conflict theory in sociology seeks explanations of conflicting behaviour of all kinds, not simply in the confrontation between some individuals and a set of apparently universally accepted social rules, but in the development of and changes in institutions and social structures such that a whole range of authority-subject relationships determine action. In this event Turk (1969) has said that

> The study of criminality becomes the study of relations between the statuses and roles of *legal authorities* — creators, interpreters, and enforcers of right/wrong standards for individuals in the political collectivity — and those of subjects — acceptors or resistors but not makers of such law creating, interpreting and enforcing decisions. [p. 35]

However, whilst seeing some aspects of new conflict theory as an advance, Taylor *et al.* (1973) are otherwise critical since

> ... such a conception undermines or understresses an alternative view of men as purposive creators and innovators of action. In particular, it leads to an approach to crime in which action is merely and simply a product of powerful interest or unequal society — as opposed to being a product of purposive individual or collective action taken to resolve such inequalities of power and interest. It tends to suggest that one can only be a deviant when one is seen or described as a deviant by the powerful interests of the day or when one is in a disadvantaged position in such an unequal society. In so doing the conflict approach is in danger of withdrawing integrity and purpose — or idiosyncracy — from men: and, thus, is close to erecting a view of crime as non purposive (or pathological) reaction to external circumstances. [p. 217]

Other sociological work has, however, paid particular attention to the 'external circumstance', and far from seeing crime as a reaction to it has demonstrated the interactive nature of criminal behaviour and society's reaction. Erickson (1962) said that

> Deviance is not a property *inherent* in certain kinds of behaviour; it is a property *conferred upon* these forms by the audiences which directly or indirectly witness them. Sociologically, then, the critical variable is the social audience. . . since it is the audience which eventually decides whether any given action or actions will become a visible case of deviation.

Whether our interest is particularly in psychological or sociological studies of crime, it is clear that ultimately attempts to explain crime rates must be seen in the context of the secular increase in rates. If it is concluded that an important explanatory feature of the criminal behaviour studied is broken homes or, say, slow speed of physiological reaction to stress, then it must surely be necessary to ask how the incidence of these things is related to the rate of change of acquisition of a criminal label. Are people with slow speeds of reaction to stress increasing in numbers, or are they for some reason, which must be explained, coming more to the attention of the police?

Whilst accepting with Taylor *et al.* the need for a fully social theory of deviance, I shall argue that their insistence on a theory to explain all deviance has run ahead of particular and necessarily detailed examination of what they call 'the actual act' of crime itself. Much research has been carried out on the actual act, and certain aspects of this work serve as indicators of the detailed consideration that is necessary in order to make much-needed links between the various kinds of theories.

The first place to seek explanations is the front line of the official agencies, namely the police, who have to decide then and there which acts constitute an offence and which do not. In their study of US police work Piliavin and Briar (1964) found that

> . . . police officers actually had access to only very limited information about boys at the time they had to decide what to do with them. In the field, officers typically had no data concerning the past offence records, school performance, family situation, or personal adjustment of apprehended youths. . . First both the decision made in the field. . . and the decision made at the station. . . were based largely on clues which emerged from interaction between the officer and the youth, clues from which the officer inferred the youth's character.

These authors report differential treatment of suspects according to whether youths were felt to be cooperative or not, whether they were negro or not, and on a whole range of other personal characteristics. Another US study of policemen at work found that only 15 per cent of encounters between patrol officers and juvenile suspects resulted in arrest, and showed the importance of the role of the complainant. In that study Black and Reiss (1970) found that 78 per cent of police-juvenile encounters were initiated by complaints, and they concluded that whilst police behaviour followed the same *patterns* for negro and white juveniles, *differential outcomes* arose from differences in complainant's behaviour.

Simmons (1969) noted how the policeman's freedom to interpret the information immediately available to him can be used in an interpretation of the law that is not so much related to the immediate social circumstances as to the policeman's views of a particular kind of person or event.

> A minor infraction becomes a pretext for dismissing or failing to promote someone who is disapproved of on other grounds. Since virtually everyone can be found guilty of some infractions the official has a ready means of dealing with someone deemed unsuitable or someone he and his public disapprove of. California officials have, for example, harassed hippy communes and psychedelic shops by rigorously enforcing obscure ordinances. A bearded, bell-wearing youth was arrested before my eyes on a Southern California beach for 'playing a musical instrument in public without a licence'. [p. 108]

As well as his information about the immediate situation the policeman will have a concept of crime that ranks offences into levels of importance and that conditions the amount of police time that it is legitimate to spend on them. There seems to be no published research in this area, but from observation it looks as if large-scale robbery and fraud, and violence are ranked as 'most important', and both to some extent considered to be the *real* stuff of police work rather than the 'lighter weight' housebreaking, shoplifting and traffic offences. McClintock and Avison (1968) noted the high percentage of crimes of violence and of murder reported as 'cleared up', and Walker (1971) concluded that 'the reason is partly that the police take more trouble over personal violence than over most other sorts of crime' (p. 32). Conversely, larceny from unattended vehicles is a 'type of crime which the police rightly regard as little more than a nuisance' (p. 32). In discussing measures of police efficiency Walker recommends the selection of offences 'which the police are known to take seriously' (p. 32). It is common knowledge that police interest in a reported offence will not be stinted, for example, for public violence or bank robbery, but may well be low for a break-in at a private house, and even be denied for a traffic accident that has involved law infraction but that does not involve personal injury. This postulated concept of importance also contains an element of what might be called 'social offensiveness' grading, in the sense that the active prosecution of some sorts of crime depends on the social circumstances in which they occur. For example, fighting will more readily attract an assault charge if it occurs in the street or other public place than if it takes place in the factory, or between neighbours, or in the home.

If it is reasonable to postulate a police grading of the importance of offences, then we may assume there to be something similar in the minds of others who are not policemen for this concept to work at all. It is suggested that the lay public also grade offences on a similar scale of importance, as may be seen both in selective press coverage of court proceedings and occurrences of offences, and in the public reporting of crime. Support for this view has been demonstrated by Banks *et al.* (1975) who asked their English and Welsh sample

> . . . which of 18 offences they considered to be serious. Practically all agreed that murder, robbery with violence, sexual offences against children, cruelty to children, indecently assaulting a woman, and causing death by dangerous driving was serious crime. Manslaughter was considered to be serious by 86%, and well over half the informants thought that deliberately damaging property, fraud and housebreaking were serious offences. A substantial minority considered that breaking into a factory was serious too. One third thought that stealing was serious, although this proportion varied according to the socio-economic group and level of education of the informant, with half the top socio-economic group considering it serious. Less than a third thought that fighting, taking away a motor vehicle without the owner's consent, being drunk and disorderly, stealing by finding, travelling without paying the fare, or vagrancy were serious (the last two were thought to be serious by only 10% of respondents). People who admitted having travelled by train or bus themselves without paying the fare were less likely than others to consider this a serious offence. Similarly, those who admitted having taken something from work to which they were not really entitled were less likely to think that stealing 'by finding' was serious.

Similarly Rossi *et al.* (1974), Sparks *et al.* (1977) and Walker (1979) have also studied public attitudes to crime and its seriousness, and have reported a surprisingly high degree of consensus in concepts of seriousness as well as its variation by sex, social class and certain other characteristics. Apart from the academic work, many large stores and libraries accept that there will be an inevitable amount of theft by both staff and customers, and they are much less likely to report a 'walk in' theft or a 'shoplifting' than the discovery of a break-in. Martin (1962) observed that businessmen draw a line between 'reasonable pilfering' and theft, and Borrell and Cashinella (who estimated in 1975 that the annual value of theft from shops by customers was 100 million pounds *per annum* and by staff was 200 million pounds *per annum*) report a director of an Oxford Street store to have said that it is

> . . . virtually impossible to stop this sort of thing happening. We are just having to live with it. I agree it is a sad reflection on the integral honesty of not only the customers, but our employees as well. But many of them just regard pilfering as one of the perks of the job. It is almost an expected part of their wage packet, a sort of tax-free bonus. [p. 107]

Walker (1971) quotes an American study carried out by the National Opinion Research Centre in 1967 which found great differences in proportions of offences not notified to the police, ranging from 90 per cent of 'consumer fraud' and 63 per cent of 'larceny under $50', down through 49 per cent of 'sex offences other than forcible rape' to 35 per cent of 'aggravated assaults', 35 per cent of 'robberies' and 11 per cent of 'auto thefts'. Variation in these percentages may be partly because of previous experience of differences in police attitudes towards reports of such offences and because, in the case of car thefts, of insurance claim requirements. Although many people feel indignant when they see an obvious fare dodger escape detection, or a motorist clearly breaking the speed limit, they are not very likely to report this law-breaking to the police. There is also low likelihood of reporting of petty cash offences and of shoplifting, and even though this may be ascribed to witnesses and the police not wanting to become involved in the complex process of law for such a small thing, this itself reflects an ordering of crime into things 'worth' the bother of the investigation and perhaps also a court appearance, and other things less worth reporting.

How might these concepts of relative importance of crimes originate? I shall suggest that there are basically two sources.

The first is a notion of victim involvement. People are particularly affronted or horrified, as well as fascinated, by offences in which others are the primary victims, that is when others are physically hurt or assaulted by someone else (in circumstances other than traffic accidents). Possibly the thought of it happening to them influences people to put these high victim-involvement crimes at the top of the importance of offences scale in terms of pursuing, apprehending and prosecuting the offender. I suggest that as the notion of a victim becomes more remote, and as the idea of the violation of personal space dwindles, so the 'importance' of the offence decreases until, for many, a 'victim' would seem practically incomprehensible in the case of shoplifting or fare dodging, and non-existent in the case of such motoring offences as speeding.

The second notion is that of the stereotyped image of criminals, discussed particularly cogently by Schur (1971), who quotes Lippman (1922) on opinion formation — 'we do not first see, then define, we define first and then see. . . we are told about the world before we see it. We imagine most things before we experience them. And those preconceptions, unless education has made us completely aware, govern deeply the whole process of perception.' Most people have not met, least of all known, a murderer, a rapist or a robber, but they have had plenty of opportunity to build up an image of the kind of people who become these things. As Simmons (1969) observed, 'your view of deviance derives partly from your preconceptions about human nature in general (since deviants are human beings), partly from hearsay (the vast bulk of anyone's ideas is second hand), and partly from the nature of your own personality (since you do the labelling and reacting in concrete instances)' (p. 13). Simmons carried out unstructured interviews to discover respondents' stereotyped or 'typified' images of homosexuals, beatniks, adulterers and marihuana smokers — unfortunately all forms of deviance with at most only secondary victim involvement — and concluded that a predominantly 'pariah' image was held, somewhat modified by the observer's educational experience. Such images of deviance are constantly reinforced by lay awareness of particular urban areas associated with high crime rates, by a kind of folk knowledge of the long-term adverse effects of such things as illegitimacy, working mothers, 'latchkey children' (as the press call them) and broken homes, and by the tendency for press reports of, say, violent crime to find something in the person's background to account for the behaviour — as Scheff (1966) observed they not infrequently include remarks like 'a former mental patient. . .'. Banks and her colleagues (1975) concluded from their review of surveys of public attitudes to crime that 'The main things that seem to stand out from all these surveys is the general agreement about the causes of crime. A majority of people everywhere think that crime can be attributed to lack of parental discipline, although this feeling tends to be stronger in America than in Britain.' Such stereotypes reinforce the notion of the 'differentness' of offenders from others, and I suggest that as victim involvement and personal-space violation increase so it is commonly expected that 'differentness' will also increase. This 'differentness', it should be stressed, need not necessarily be seen in mental illness terms, but in terms of social circumstances, such as those outlined above.

Some support for these proposals about the relative importance and seriousness of crimes can be drawn both from official statistics and from the self-report studies. Table 1.1 shows the great range of differences in clear-up rates as between crimes. In some instances this may be ascribed to certain features of the crime itself; for instance, as Walker (1971) said, the high clear-up rate of violence against a person is mainly because 'the victim knows his or her assailant personally' (p. 32), but this is somewhat less likely in sexual offences and in fraud and forgery, which both have relatively high clear-up rates.

The self-report studies are more difficult to evaluate since their populations are so different in respect of age, since they are drawn from US, Scandinavian and English populations, since they all ask different questions and since there is no way of knowing the amount of concealment or exaggeration that has occurred, nor yet whether the admitted act did in every case really constitute a crime. Nevertheless, they show for males the same general picture as is demonstrated by the English and Welsh official statistics of crimes known to the police. Theft, damage to property and disorderly conduct are most frequently reported, while sexual offences, violence and robbery are relatively less often confessed. Ever since the estimates of unofficial delinquency made by case workers on the Cambridge-Somerville study, in which it was shown that of all unofficial delinquent acts reported 6.2 per cent were 'serious offences' and that 12.3 per cent of official acts were similarly classified (Murphy *et al.,*

TABLE 1.1 *Indictable offences known to the police per 100,000 of the English and Welsh population, 1973-76, ranked in order of percentage cleared up*

	1973		1974		1975		1976	
	No. known	% cleared up	No. known	% cleared up	No. known	% cleared up	No. known	% cleared up
Other offences*	16	93	17	91	17	92	21	93
Fraud and forgery	225	82	238	82	250	84	244	81
Violence against the person: Homicide	1	} 87	1	} 80	1	} 81	1	} 79
Other	124		128		143		157	
Sexual offences	52	78	50	78	48	78	45	77
Theft and handling stolen goods	2031	43	2419	42	2577	41	2614	41
Robbery	15	46	18	40	23	40	24	33
Criminal damage	107	39	136	38	160	37	189	35
Burglary	800	37	983	34	1061	34	1048	34

* Other indictable offences include blackmail, other offences against public order, riot, libel, unlawful assembly, aiding suicide, treason and high treason.
Source: *Criminal Statistics*, 1973, 1974, 1975, 1976

1946), estimates and self reports of 'unofficial' delinquency have shown a similar tendency for serious offences to be relatively fewer. Wallerstein and Wyle (1947), for example, found that in reply to a postal questionnaire 11 per cent of men admitted committing robbery, 49 per cent assault and 89 per cent larceny. Clark and Wenninger (1962) in a carefully planned self-report study found that whereas 77.6 per cent of respondents admitted a minor theft and 34.7 per cent a major one, 19.9 per cent admitted to starting a fist fight, 10.7 per cent taking part in a gang fight and 3.0 per cent to 'attacking someone with the idea of killing them'. In this country Hood and Sparks (1970) quote Willcock's self-report figures of 16-20 per cent for vandalism, gang fighting and larceny, but only 1.7-3.3 per cent admitted serious offences — 'breaking and entering, fighting the police and attacking unknown persons' (p. 49); and McDonald (1969) had self reports of 'assault' from 23.3 per cent of her population and of 'petty shop lifting' from 58.1 per cent.

Belson (1968) reported very high levels of theft by teenage boys and Sparks *et al.* (1977) investigated self reports by victims. I have commented on difficulties in the interpretation of self-report studies both in this chapter and in chapter 10; generally it does seem from this body of work that crime that is either unreported by the victim and/or the offender or is technically an offence although because of the social circumstances of its occurrence is not likely to be seen as a crime (see the earlier example of marital quarrels), what, in short, is known as the 'dark statistic' of crime may be postulated as largest in those offences that attract least attention from the police, that are seen as least offensive and that have the least or no evident victim involvement. Conversely, the 'dark statistic' is apparently smallest in crimes that are most commonly seen as particularly offensive, that attract most police attention and that have evident victim involvement, with the exception of fraud. Although at first sight Sparks *et al.* (1977) seem to have shown a very large dark statistic in their London study of victims of violent crime, they included *threats* as well as acts of violence and, as they say, unreported 'crimes' of violence of this kind were on average 'far less serious' (p. 77) than those reported to the police. From the self-report studies, from the studies of police work and from the investigations of public attitudes to crime and its causes, it seems an incontrovertible conclusion that breaking the law or criminal deviance cannot be seen as a homogeneous phenomenon.

It is probably true to say that sociologists form the group that has been most constructive in pointing out the difficulties these facts raise for any kind of research that asks why people commit crimes, although they have paid relatively little attention to the importance of differentiating crime types and most attention to the operation of the systems for detecting, prosecuting and punishing offenders. However, sociologists do seem in broad agreement with others, both in research and outside the academic world, that we need to know why people break the law, although reasons for wanting to know why doubtless differ from group to group. Regrettably, the lucid and considerable sociological contribution to seeing the importance of the social context of crime has included relatively little of practical value, at least to research workers.

Somehow empirical research into why people break the law now has to take account of these findings and discussions. This study is an attempt to do this, and it uses whole life histories of a large group of people to ask why some of them committed crimes whilst others did not.

CHAPTER 2

Measuring Delinquency

INTRODUCTION

As Becker (1964) said,

> What laymen want to know about deviants is; why do they do it?...
> What is there about them that leads them to do forbidden things?
> Scientific research has tried to find answers to these questions. In
> so doing it has accepted the common sense assumption that there
> is something inherently deviant (qualitatively distinct) about acts
> that break. . .social rules. It has also accepted the common sense
> assumption that the deviant act occurs because some characteristic
> of the person who commits it makes it necessary or inevitable that
> he should. Scientists do not ordinarily question that label 'deviant'
> when it is applied to particular acts or people but rather take it as
> given. In so doing, they accept the values of the group making the
> judgement. [pp. 11-12]

This study has not accepted 'deviance' as a workable research
concept. In looking at associations between offending and the life
history data of the study population the aim has been to re-examine
some of the associations usually found in criminological studies, and
in doing so to make use of the relatively recent views of such workers
as Cicourel and Becker and Schur who have also questioned the use
of the label 'deviance'. It has also been possible to some extent to
examine the contention that some kinds of people or people in
certain kinds or combinations of kinds of circumstances are more
likely, in any event, to be seen as behaving wrongly or less tolerably
than others, and thus more likely to be punished for it.

This study's claim to make a contribution to the understanding of
what delinquency is, is based on its collection of life history data.
This has the unique advantage of being collected on a wide range of
medical, social and psychological topics from a large and representative national population at intervals of two years or less from

birth throughout their childhood, adolescence and early adult life. Thus, claims can be tested about the power of this experience or that event in the aetiology of delinquency that have been made in studies based on smaller samples and using recollected data. Much criminological research has been concerned to look back over what delinquents can remember or are prepared to report of their earlier lives, and has then compared their reports with those of non-delinquents and drawn conclusions about causes of delinquency and about its prevention and early detection. Kagan (1976) has observed that a concept of continuity between events in early life and behaviour in later life, or what he calls 'psychological epigenesis', is practically traditional in psychology, but that relatively little interest has been taken in the demonstration of its validity.

> . . . psychological epigenesis deals with the necessary relations between a set of processes or performances at one time and a successive set at some time in the future. Western psychologists are friendly towards a strong form of epigenesis due, in large part, to the theories of Freud and Piaget. For example, some psychologists believe there is a necessary continuity or relation between fear of parental punishment at age 3 and an internalized conscience at age 10 or a continuity between the opportunity to manipulate objects during infancy and a subsequent appearance of symbolic thought at 2 years of age. However attractive the epigenetic hypotheses, they are, in the main, neither supported nor disconfirmed by empirical data. [p. 103]

A study such as the present one, having collected information about a large population of individuals before any of them, either boys or girls, became delinquent, should be able to make certain unique contributions to the study of delinquency. Most notably it can test out the epigenetic hypotheses about associations between early life events and later delinquency.

Since the relatively few studies that have investigated recollection find it to be an important cause of distortion it is worthwhile to consider the particular value of prospectively collected data. In these studies straightforward memory lapse has often been noted. For example, in preparations for the US National Health Survey Nisselson and Woolsey (1959) found that incidence rates of illness dropped as time away from interview increased. Gray (1955) noted that informants readily placed events (sick leave) much nearer in time to the interview than they really occurred, and Cartwright (1963), in a carefully planned morbidity study in which general practitioners kept records of consultations and patients were interviewed, found that there was an error of 'between 5% and 15% in both reporting and recording'. Again in a morbidity enquiry, in this cohort, Douglas and Blomfield (1956) found that two years after the event 7.4 per cent of mothers failed to recall that their two-year-old children had had either measles or whooping cough. More recent work by Yarrow *et al.* (1970) has demonstrated, as some of the quoted authors suggest, that the problem is not simply one of memory error in relation to time elapsed. In their study of recollections of childhood of both mothers and children, they found that the amount of time elapsed was not 'an overwhelming factor in shaping recall'. They discovered evidence of systematic distortion of recall of mothers and children over a period of up to thirty years, and found that '. . . when the recalled past was systematically different from the contemporaneous record, informants who were involved in "cold" mother/child relationships systematically reshaped their pasts, seeing them in less favoured or desirable perspective' (p. 48). Distortion effects related to father's occupational status and own educational aspirations were noted by Kayser (1974) in student reporting of parental occupation and education; he found correct reporting of only 71.0 per cent of father's occupations, 52.9 per cent of father's education and 62.0 per cent of mother's education.

One sure way to avoid the problems of recall is to use a longitudinal research design, observing research subjects over time and recording facts and attitudes contemporaneously. Goldstein (1969) has discussed the definition of a longitudinal study in these terms:

> The distinction between 'prospective' and 'longitudinal' studies seems to be a little uncertain. According to Yerushalmy, the prospective study is usually concerned with 'outcome' (the value of a selected characteristic measured on the last occasion in a 'deviant' group of individuals subject to some form of treatment). For example, a study of the adult intelligence (outcome) in a group of illegitimate children (a 'deviant' group) who have been adopted (treatment). A control group is usually present. The true 'longitudinal' study is defined as one in which the whole 'pattern' of development is of interest, and it is usually concerned with a sample of 'normal' individuals.

There have been a number of long-term follow-up studies of children that have been particularly concerned with delinquency. Some have selected a group of delinquents and matched them with controls and carried out follow-up studies comparing careers of the two groups.

For example, the Cambridge-Somerville study, which followed up the careers of 325 matched pairs of 'delinquency prone' boys from 1939 to 1945, counselled one boy and not the other within pairs and compared criminal records (Powers and Witmer, 1951). The boys were contacted later and their criminal records again compared (McCord *et al.,* 1959). The Gluecks followed up a sample of 500 boys for fifteen years, delinquents matched with controls (S. Glueck and E. Glueck, 1940). In Germany, Fuchs-Kamp (1929) examined delinquency, amongst other things, in boys eighteen years after their release from reform school, and in Sweden, Arctander (1936) traced occupational histories of delinquents matched both with boys receiving child guidance and with a group of controls. Other studies have concentrated on disturbed children for follow-up. There have been three follow-up studies of children who attended child guidance clinics in the USA (Morris *et al.,* 1954; Roff, 1961; and Robins, 1966), and one in Sweden (Otterstrom, 1946) to examine their propensity to later criminal behaviour.

Most of these studies, with the exception of the Cambridge-Somerville investigation, have in common the fact that the base population was not in any sense normal, in that they comprised either delinquents or disturbed children and, as West (1969) has pointed out, they therefore risk 'masking the effect of the interaction between factors which occurs in a natural setting' (p. 5). West himself is following up a sample of 411 boys living in London, beginning before the age of criminal responsibility at age 8 or 9 years. As he says:

> By taking an unselected group of normal children, and studying the whole range of natural variation one has the chance to assess more realistically the relative importance of various background factors in the genesis of delinquency as they operate together in real life. Furthermore, by investigating on these lines, one finds out the actual incidence in a particular segment of the community of the different kinds of personal and social handicap which are believed to favour delinquency. [p. 5]

THE PRESENT STUDY

The study reported here has four important advantages in addition to those enjoyed by West's study:

(1) the present follow-up was begun at birth;

(2) the children were born in all parts of England, Wales and Scotland and constitute a representative national sample;

(3) the numbers are large enough to permit both the examination of different crime types and the use of multivariate statistical analysis; and

(4) the investigation has been concerned not solely with the search for 'criminogenic' factors but with a wide range of topics in health, education and family life.

All the children taking part in this study were born in one week in March 1946 (3rd to 9th). They were selected from the total population of births occurring in that week in England, Wales and Scotland by the inclusion of all legitimate single births to wives of non-manual and agricultural workers, and one in four of all legitimate single births to wives of manual workers (classified according to the Family Census of 1946 — Royal Commission on Population). Since that time the survey population of 5362 children has been studied at intervals of not less than two years up until its members were aged 26 years. Information has been collected about birth circumstances, growth, development, illness, social circumstances and home environment in the pre-school years, and then again, together with the school progress and behaviour data, throughout the school years. (See Appendix for a note on data collection.) After leaving school, information on career selection and unemployment, further and higher education, marriage and income has also been collected. The study therefore conforms to Goldstein's (1969) definition of a true longitudinal study as one that is concerned with a whole pattern of development rather than with a specific issue. Thus for each child in the study there exists a life history unencumbered with the problem of long-term recollection and therefore going some way to meet Schur's (1973) requirement of the need to recognise 'that human behaviour emerges out of continuous processes of social interaction' (p. 136).

This mass of information constitutes a unique opportunity to study law breakers, and to make many kinds of comparison between them and other Survey members who did not break the law. There is, however, what may be seen as a drawback, in that information on law-breaking in the cohort is confined to 'official' data; no self-report information on offending has ever been collected. Information about conviction for Standard List offences committed by the sample

between ages 8 and 21 years was supplied by the Criminal Record
Office at New Scotland Yard and by the Home Office Statistical
Department; child care officers and probation officers also supplied
information, including data about cautions. Some information about
the circumstances as well as the official classification of crime is
available, but it exists only in a non-standardised form and only for
some of the offences. This study is concerned with all the information
on offending in England and Wales. Scottish offenders were omitted
since there were some difficulties of definition involved in considering them together with English and Welsh offenders in one and
the same group, and since the method of collecting information in
Scotland left it open to doubt that all offences by Scottish Survey
members were discovered. The population used is a sub-sample,
consisting of all boys and girls alive and resident in England and
Wales on their eighth birthday, which at that time (1954) was the age
of commencement of criminal responsibility. The total number of
boys selected to be the sub-sample population was 2196, and they
represent 78.0 per cent of the total original National Survey
population of 2815 males. The sub-sample of English and Welsh
girls was 2035 or 80.0 per cent of all girls.

Representativeness of the data

Before discussing how best such data may be used, it is important to
ascertain how accurate a representation of the whole national
experience of offending by persons of this age is given by information
on officially recognised offending in this cohort. It cannot be a
completely accurate representation since on drawing the sample
population from the whole birth week illegitimate and multiple
births were excluded, and unlike the selection of only one in four of
manual workers this cannot be compensated for by weighting
(weighting is achieved by multiplying each of the manual workers'
children by four). The sample also excludes immigrants arriving
after the selected birth week, but is itself depleted by emigration and
death. By the end of 1966, when the study population was aged 20
years and 10 months, losses by emigration were 416 (7.8 per cent) and
by death were 268 (5.0 per cent). Refusal to cooperate had risen to a
maximum of only 5.8 per cent by age 26 years.

In these sub-samples, delinquents were identified and defined as all those who appeared before courts and were found guilty of an indictable offence(s) or of a non-indictable offence(s) and dealt with summarily, or who were cautioned by the police for such an offence.

TABLE 2.1 *The distribution of male offenders, observed and weighted*

	No offences	Non-indictable offences	One indictable offences	More than one indictable offence	Total (=100%)
Observed	84.7	4.7	7.2	3.4	2196
Weighted	82.1	4.9	8.2	4.7	5124

Of the 336 boys who were so defined (15.3 per cent of the total sub-sample), thirty-five were cautioned only, three of them on two separate occasions. Of the forty delinquent girls (2.0 per cent of the total sub-sample), thirty-eight appeared before a court and two were cautioned. In the weighted sample, 17.9 per cent of boys appeared before the courts or were cautioned, and so did 2.5 per cent of girls. Table 2.1 shows the distribution of male offenders and non-offenders, both observed and weighted to compensate for the sampling bias. (Female offenders are discussed in chapter 10.)

The representativeness of this population was found to be good by comparing the incidence of guilt findings in the total population of England and Wales, in the National Survey weighted population and in the National Survey observed population (Wadsworth, 1975). There are slight differences between the incidence of delinquency in the National Survey weighted population and the English and Welsh population; these are likely to be the result of factors discussed above and may also be because the National Survey population 'at risk' of offending is exactly known, but this is not so for the officially published statistics which are an estimate. As well as showing a close similarity between the national figures and the rates of offending by the sub-sample, this population has two further advantages. Not only is it geographically representative of the national population, but it is also of sufficient size for there to be some breakdown of law-breaking into types of offences, the importance of which was discussed in the first chapter.

Uses of these data

The advantage of contemporaneously collected and detailed data on many aspects of life from birth onwards is rarely available to researchers, and we are particularly fortunate in this, and in having such data on a national and representative population. Since the information is so comprehensive and unencumbered with the problem of recollection, it has been used to examine the relevance of data usually considered basic in aetiological research and to test claims about the power in delinquency studies of this widely used method of explanation. Most studies of delinquency have sought to explain offending by way of the aetiological method, that is by looking back over as many events as possible in offenders' life histories to find experiential and personal ways in which offenders differ from non-offenders, and many would agree with West and Farrington (1973) that 'rational preventive action ought to be based on aetiological theory' (p. 204). However, findings have been questionable when aetiological research has had to rely on memory for its data. Recent disenchantment with aetiological research has also been not simply with these aspects of its method, but with its particularly selective approach to data that might be relevant and its lack of specificity about why the data were selected.

Many analysts have not explained their assumptions in the choice of variables from the universe of all possible variables and this has led to ambiguity and lack of clarity in their interpretations and discussions of findings. For example, it is usually not specified whether such information as social class is collected or is being interpreted as a shorthand description of life style, an indicator of family income or a measure of the father's education achievements or whether it is used simply because, by observation, there seems to be an over-representation of a particular social class in populations of officially defined offenders. Similarly, family size is usually described, but is this because of its assumed association with relative poverty, or because of the 'social visibility' of children from such families or because it may have an alienating effect on some children by reducing the available maternal attention?

National Survey data have been used to elucidate some of these problems. Assumptions about the choice of variables and their use in this study are discussed in each chapter, and the population's size has allowed the use of multivariate statistical analysis so that the interrelationships of the information can be examined to discover, for example, which particular aspect of family size accounted for its association with delinquency.

This information can also be helpful in the problem of translating research findings into proposals for some kind of action. Here, at least, the aetiological studies merit less adverse comment, even though some of the proposals for action may not be widely seen as acceptable. This relative lack of hard propositions may be because of the basically discouraging nature of findings, which can be masked by reference to statistical significances rather than presentation of all aspects of the results. In this study, for example, there is a clear association between large family size and delinquency; its statistical significance indicated that the likelihood of this difference occurring by chance was less than one in a thousand. Forty-one (70 per cent) male recidivists came from large families (i.e., had three or more siblings) as compared with two recidivists (3 per cent) who were only children, but nevertheless it is still true that 76 per cent of children who lived in large families *did not* become delinquent. Comparable findings exist for social class.

It is clear, therefore, that the practical usefulness of knowing about an association between large family size and delinquency does not lie in seeing large families as a group amongst which potential delinquents may be readily detected, but that this association is useful for the direction of more specific research effort. This study's population size and its mass of information give the opportunity to examine various interpretations of family size and to look for evidence to support them among those predicted as delinquents but who were in fact not so — the false positives. Were there, for example, any ways in which those who came from large families and were delinquent, were different from those who came from large families but were not delinquent?

But how can these various advantages help when the only information available on offending is 'official' information? It will certainly be a disadvantage insofar as the group of officially defined non-offenders will actually contain those who, if asked, would report that they had broken the law. However, if this information had been collected its interpretation would be difficult. Completeness of reporting would be unknowable but certainly there would be both under-reporting and exaggeration in reporting. There would, too, be no indication of the social context of these self-reported offences and, as already discussed in the first chapter, it is the social context and the witnesses, if any, that form the first essential stage in deciding whether an action is to be defined as a crime. Thus, a question that in a self-report study takes the form 'have you ever been involved in a fist fight?' will give little information about whether this event forms part of the 'dark statistic'. There will be no way of knowing whether it did not become officially classified as an offence because there was no one else present, because none of those who saw the event thought it worth reporting to the police, or because the police were called but decided not to prosecute. It is important to remember that both lay and police witnesses will be influenced in their decisions to inform or prosecute by the kinds of people taking part in the event as well as by the nature of the event. These difficulties would be equally present in the interpretation of 'have you ever taken goods from a shop and avoided payment?' but answers to this sort of question can be classified according to the reported value of the goods taken, so that their 'dark value' may be established. Without information on the social context of events it is very difficult to interpret either self reports of events that might be offensive or even official reports of offending.

But the recent sociological work gives us enough information to group offences. We can, therefore, get together a group of offences that the studies show are commonly felt to be 'minor', i.e., not much worth reporting. Obviously those officially prosecuted for committing such offences will not represent anything like all those who actually committed them, but in offences where there seems to be common agreement about 'seriousness' a much better representation of offenders amongst those officially designated as offenders will be achieved. If this could be done in the present study, and if the assumptions about representativeness behind such a classification were correct, then it would be particularly interesting to look at those who had gone so much against conventional views as to commit a 'serious' crime. In fact, we might expect to be able to differentiate 'minor' delinquents from non-delinquents with practically no success, but to find considerable differences between 'serious' delinquents and others because of their willingness to behave in a way that seems generally agreed to be least tolerable.

A scale was therefore drawn up to take account of the arguments already put forward concerning adjudged social offensiveness and acceptability of offences and their personal-space violation and victim involvement. Some precedent exists for a scale of tolerability, but mainly in the work of those concerned to measure changes in levels or amounts of criminality in a society rather than, as is the present requirement, to differentiate individuals from one another. In their review of attempts at measurements, Sellin and Wolfgang (1964) cite the concern of many workers with '. . . both the conception which the population has of the punishable nature of the crime and its seriousness in general, as well as its detectability' (p. 35). In the construction of their own index to establish weights indicative of 'seriousness', Sellin and Wolfgang submitted some details of hypothetical offences to panels of university students, police officers, criminal and juvenile court judges, those selected for jury duty, victims of criminal or delinquent acts and samples drawn from the general population. They concluded that 'a pervasive social agreement about what is serious and what is not appeared to emerge, and this agreement transcends simple qualitative concordance; it extends to the estimated numerical degree of seriousness of these offences' (p. 268). More recent work both in this country and in the United States using representative samples of the population also concludes that there is a considerable degree of agreement on perceived seriousness of crimes (see, for example, Rossi *et al.*, 1974; Sparks *et al.*, 1977; and Walker, 1979). In their scale of seriousness, Sellin and Wolfgang

> . . . grouped the offences . . . into two main classes with appropriate subdivisions. In the first class we placed offences that involved the infliction of some physical harm on the victim or caused the loss or destruction of property. In the second class we placed offences against persons that did not result in any harm to them or to their property, offences that disturbed public order, the 'juvenile status' offences, and those of a consensual or conspiratorial nature. All the forms of juvenile conduct that lead to police intervention are thus included in the two classes except curfew violations, which were excluded from our study from the beginning. [p. 148]

Furthermore, they say that

> An event should not be evaluated solely in terms of such injuries or losses. Account must also be taken of certain factors of the event that aggravate it. A theft from a person, regardless of the amount taken, is aggravated if the victim is intimidated, especially if a dangerous weapon is used for that purpose, and the use of such a weapon to accomplish a rape also aggravates that event. Furthermore, theft or damage to property in a building or an assaultive event inside a building is aggravated if force was used to enter the premises. The scale in question takes account of both the components and the aggravating factors of an event. [p. 297]

FIGURE 2.1 *The social acceptability of crime scale*

0	1	2	3	4
No delinquency known	'Minor' offences that are unlikely to be socially unacceptable, and that are victimless and not acquisitive, e.g. speeding.	Loss of property but no breaking to achieve this. May be impulsive. No personal injury or primary victim, e.g. receiving, taking a motor vehicle without the owner's consent.	Loss of property and damage to property involving breaking. Unlikely to be so impulsive. No personal injury of victim involved, e.g. theft of vehicle, breaking and entering, malicious (now criminal) damage.	All kinds of injuries and assaults on others, except the result of traffic accidents, e.g. rape, grievous bodily harm.

No victim involvement and no personal-space violation. Most socially acceptable.

→

Most victim involvement, most personal-space violation. Most socially unacceptable.

In the present study the concept of a scaling of offences, in ways other than the basic legal statistical categorisation of indictable/non-indictable offences, has been influenced both by the work of Sellin and Wolfgang, by the work of McClintock and Avison (1968) and by the studies quoted in the first chapter. Although these workers all seem in remarkably close agreement about the grading of offences, the grading attempted here is, unlike that of Sellin and Wolfgang, in no way claimed to be reproducible, since it covers only those offences committed by Survey members. It is intended that this scale should represent four basic groupings of general social intolerance or acceptability of offending, and it is therefore referred to as the social acceptability of crime scale (SAC scale). It has no value higher than ordinal.

Figure 2.1 gives the five points of the scale and the reasons for including offences in each category. As in Sellin and Wolfgang's work, it has not been possible to categorise every single event, the main reason being that sometimes no element of offensiveness is present, in that there was evidence of mutual consent or certainly no indication of aggression between the offender and the person who would otherwise be the victim. The list of the five types of offence encountered and not categorised in the scale is given in the Appendix, together with the offences in each of the categories.

Each offender was allocated to the highest possible score category on the scale, using all the offences he had been known to commit. Thus, even though the person might have committed a number of shoplifting and burglary offences, one assault or rape placed him in category 4 on the scale. The distribution of offenders on this scale is given in Table 2.2, and Table 2.3 shows the distribution of indictable offenders on the scale.

Those who score 4 on the SAC scale have behaved in a way that is generally least acceptable and that in prison populations sometimes

TABLE 2.2 *The distribution of male offenders on the social acceptability of crime scale, observed and weighted*

| | Social acceptability of crime scale | | | | | Total (=100%) |
	0	1	2	3	4	
Observed	84.9	2.3	7.0	4.0	1.8	2191
Weighted	82.3	2.4	8.2	4.8	2.2	5113

TABLE 2.3 *The distribution of once only and of recidivist indictable male offenders on the social acceptability of crime scale, observed and weighted (in brackets)*

Indictable offenders	Social acceptability of crime scale				Total (=100%)
	1	2	3	4	
One offence	*	57.7	30.1	12.2	156
	—	(59.0)	(28.5)	(12.5)	(417)
More than one offence	*	29.3	46.7	24.0	75
	—	(32.5)	(45.3)	(22.2)	(243)

attracts the disgust of other kinds of offenders. This sort of behaviour least of all mirrors any other kind, unlike, as Merton (1957) pointed out, the similarities between acquisitive crime (scored here as 2 or 3) and normal business methods. It is, however, important to remember that offences committed by this sample are of the kind committed by males aged 8 to 20 years. As West (1967) said:

> It is safe to say that, in England, although young persons go in for crimes legally classified as serious, notably breaking and entering, compared with older offenders their scale of operations is usually more limited, their techniques more primitive and their organisation less professional, especially so in the case of juveniles. [p. 20]

The differences are important not only in respect of acquisitive crime, but also for offences against the person. The twenty-nine boys who committed violent (other than sexual) offences were convicted on twenty-one charges of assault and actual bodily harm, and on only four of grievous bodily harm and four of assault with intent to rob. The seventeen boys who committed sexual offences (one boy committed both a violent and a sexual offence) were convicted on four charges of indecent exposure, nine of indecent assaults of various kinds, one of inciting children to commit acts of indecency, one of unlawful sexual intercourse, and on only one of rape, one of bestiality and one of buggery. For the sexual offenders this was more often the one and only offence committed (ten out of the seventeen), whereas this was the case for only eight of the twenty-nine violent offenders. McClintock (1963) has pointed out the importance of differentiating between violent offences committed in the course of acquisitive crime and those committed by themselves, and in this population only five boys committed a violent offence in pursuit of acquisitive crime, but seventeen of the twenty-nine violent offenders had at some other time also committed acquisitive crime.

How can this scale be any more helpful than the classification of offences into indictable and non-indictable categories, when the social acceptability of crime scale itself also only uses official data? Will it help in a situation where there is no guarantee — on either of these two scales — that those labelled offenders represent all who have ever broken the law and that those labelled non-offenders represent another distinct population who have never broken the law?

Self-report studies show that an extremely high proportion of the population commit offences that have been scored with 1 on the SAC scale and that very many commit those scored with 2 on this scale (see chapter 1). Their findings, the official statistics on police clear-up rates, the studies of policemen at work and of public attitudes to seriousness of crime all indicate that people who commit these sorts of offences are not considered to be particularly different from people who do not, and that those who are convicted as offenders for such infractions are in a sense the 'unlucky' ones who have been caught perhaps because of a particular police concern with this sort of offence at this point in time, or because their dress or demeanour made them more susceptible to police or bystander or victim interests. Of themselves these offences are not at all likely to make others feel sufficient indignation to press for prosecution. In this investigation it is not expected that any significant factors will be found to differentiate non-offenders from offenders in categories 1 and 2 on the SAC scale. On the other hand, if the arguments for classification of offenders in categories 3 and 4 are correct, then significant differentiating factors are to be expected between these offenders and non-offenders. This is for two reasons. First, because these are offences that attract most police interest and effort and are relatively most abhorrent to both victims and others. The population constituting these offenders is therefore likely to suffer least the 'contamination' of offender groups by non-offenders and of non-offender groups by offenders. Second, differences may be expected because with the demonstrably popular weight of opinion against such offenders it is reasonable to expect some clues as to why they have at some time behaved in this deviant way.

The following chapters describe the extent of delinquency in this population, using these two measures, and search for differentiation between offenders and non-offenders chronologically through all the life history data. Boys and girls are studied separately before being discussed together in the concluding chapter.

CHAPTER 3

Social Class and the Age and Treatment of Male Offenders

Introduction

Probably the fiercest and most commonly recurring of all discussions concerning delinquency and crime has been about social-class differences, about the interpretation of their meaning in the social distribution of offending, their role in the selection of accused persons for prosecution and their place in decision about punishment or rehabilitation of the convicted. As Schur (1973) has said,

> In our society [American], lower class children more than middle class ones, black children more than white ones, and boys more than girls, face high probabilities. . . not only of engaging in rule-violation in the first place, but also of becoming enmeshed in official negative labelling processes. By the same token, their social positions afford them fewer resources with which to withstand the degrading consequences of such labelling. [pp. 125-6]

Social class is, of course, of common concern to all kinds of theorists not only as a shorthand description of life style but also because for those in the non-manual or middle classes 'departure from established norms is far less likely to bring the non-conformist into collision with the criminal law' (Morris, 1957, p. 167). This fact has been well demonstrated by the self-report studies and by much of the research into police methods.

Social Class

The incidence of delinquency and its relationship with the occupation of fathers when boys were aged 15 years shows considerable

28

differences between sons of professional and salaried workers (6.8 per cent delinquent) and those of all other non-manual workers (15.5 per cent), the latter being more often delinquent by way of both indictable and non-indictable offences and more often recidivists. Among the manual workers the sons of the unskilled had the highest incidence of delinquency (22.9 per cent) and those of agricultural workers the lowest (15.3 per cent), and they were least often recidivists (classified according to the Family Census of 1946 — Royal Commission on Population — but with the addition of the sub-division of manual workers into skill levels; see J.W.B. Douglas and J.M. Blomfield (1958) pp. 29-36). This static concept of social class, namely the socioeconomic position of the father when boys were aged 15 years, is not always the appropriate expression of class in a longitudinal study. By age 14 years practically half (46.1 per cent) of the delinquent boys had already commited an offence, and it may well have been that their social class changed between age of offending and age 15 years. Indeed, we already know that in the total National Survey population '43% of fathers moved out of their original occupational groups, and some passed through several different groups' while the Survey child was aged 0-11 years (Douglas, 1964). Therefore, in this study, a social grouping has been used that takes into account the socioeconomic origins and education of both the boy's parents, as well as the socioeconomic status of the father when the Survey child was aged 11 years — by this time only 7.5 per cent of delinquents had committed an offence. This grouping has four categories. The top two, called upper-middle and lower-middle class, encompass all whose fathers' occupations were currently non-manual and if this was not known the occupation at the birth of this child was used. The upper-middle-class population has at least one parent educated to secondary school level or above and from a middle-class family of origin, and the lower-middle class comprises all other non-manual workers. The bottom two are called upper-manual and lower-manual working classes and encompass all who were currently manual workers; if not known when the Survey child was 11 years, the occupation at the time of the child's birth was used. Upper-manual working-class families had a manual worker father and either the mother or the father or both had a secondary school education, and one or both of them were brought up in a middle-class family. Lower-manual working-class families had a manual worker father and both parents had only elementary school education and were brought up in manual working-class families. Details of the composition of this scale, which was first devised by Douglas (1964) are given in the Appendix, and it is referred to throughout as *social group*. As Douglas *et al.* (1966) noted, 'this classification has the merit that, by the very nature of its derivation, it does not change from year to year'.

TABLE 3.1   *Social group and the social acceptability of crime scale*

Social group	0 no crime	1	2	3	4	Total (=100%)
		Social acceptability of crime scale				
Upper-middle	96.0	1.6	2.0	0.4	–	251
Lower-middle	88.3	2.5	5.6	2.5	1.2	691
Upper-manual	87.6	1.7	5.5	3.2	2.0	348
Lower-manual	78.1	2.7	10.0	6.5	2.7	901

$X^2=71.6$ with 9 d.f. $p<.001$ (adding SAC scores 3 and 4 together)

TABLE 3.2   *Social group and social acceptability of crime scale scores of the population of offenders*

Social group	1	2	3	4	Total (=100%)
	Social acceptability of crime scale				
All non-manual	23.1	48.4	19.8	8.8	91
All manual	12.5	45.4	29.2	12.9	240

$X^2=8.06$ with 3 d.f. $p<.05$

In Table 3.1 the SAC scale is related to social group, and the relationship is statistically significant in the expected manner, that is with increasing proportions of delinquents as social group falls. But, if just the population of offenders is considered then, as Table 3.2 shows, the statistical significance of this relationship is considerably less, and there are really only notably more manual than non-manual group offenders in SAC categories 3 and 4.

Social mobility

Consideration of socioeconomic group change between the father's job at the time of the birth of the Survey member and the paternal grandfather's most recent occupation showed that significantly more indictable offences were committed by boys in families where there had been no change, and significantly fewer offences occurred where there had been any kind of change, regardless of its direction. Social movement was, however, not related to any particular type of later delinquency. During the first fifteen years of their Survey child's life, 37.8 per cent of fathers changed their socioeconomic status at least once in some way between the groups professional and salaried, other non-manual, skilled manual, and semi- and unskilled manual. Most of this movement took place while children were aged 0-6 years, with 65.7 per cent of upward movement and 94.6 per cent of downward movement happening during this time. If rates of delinquency are compared between non-movers and movers in each socioeconomic group a rather different picture emerges. The rates of delinquency remain related to the class of origin, whatever the movement experienced. One possible explanation is that parents who are upwardly mobile are less well versed than others in their newly acquired socioeconomic group in mobilising good legal advice for their son's defence, and perhaps not so good at persuading policemen against prosecution in favour of parental punishment, followed by the support of 'a good home'; it is also possible that schools are not quite so ready to give the good reports of these children that could help to tip the balance against prosecution. In the whole National Survey population there was also other evidence of the socially mobile carrying with them into their newly acquired class some of the characteristics of their previous class, and in the analysis of test score results, for example, Douglas (1964) observed that 'children in families that are moving up have higher measured ability than those they leave behind though rather less than those they join' (p. 41).

Age at first offence

Mean age at first offence of boys committing only non-indictable offences was 14.50 years (Standard Deviation (S.D.) 2.3), of boys committing one indictable offence it was 15.61 years (S.D. 2.9) and of boys committing more than one indictable offence 13.61 years (S.D. 2.6). There was no significant difference in mean age at first offending between social groups. Evidently minor (non-indictable) offending and first offences of recidivist indictable offenders up to age 20 years had mainly occurred by the time these boys were aged 16 years.

On the SAC scale the mean age at first offence was different only for those scoring 4. These boys were significantly older (their mean age was 15.58 years) than those in other SAC groups when they first offended, and this was because of the high mean age at first offence (17.13 years) of the sexual offenders.

Treatment of offenders

Between ages 8 and 20 years, 15.2 per cent of the delinquents spent time in some kind of custodial care after sentencing. Although there was no statistically significant relationship between social group and custodial care, the fact remains that whereas 18.4 per cent of the manual social-group delinquents spent time in custody only 9.8 per cent of non-manual delinquents did so. Proportions of those receiving custodial care rose with increasing SAC scale scores, but unfortunately numbers were too small to examine class differences in these figures. Of the 126 boys scored as 3 or 4 on the SAC scale, 34.1 per cent were at some time in custodial care. Among this group in custodial care, twelve (27.9 per cent) were from broken homes (ten of them from homes broken while the boy was aged 0-4 years), as compared with thirteen (15.7 per cent) from broken homes in the group with these SAC scores who did not have custodial care (only seven of these were from homes broken while they were aged 0-4 years). Whether this indicates bias in sentencing procedure, par-ticularly since decisions on sentencing were obviously made in many cases quite some time after the break in family life had occurred, or whether it simply reflects a tendency for individuals from these kinds of homes to commit offences more subject to custodial sentences, is a question that is reviewed in the investigation on family circumstances discussed in chapter 5. A quarter (25.3 per cent) of all delinquents were at some time under the care of a probation officer, and of these boys 34.1 per cent did not offend again — 45.4 per cent of non-manual group boys and 32.4 per cent of manual group boys. The length of time spent on probation was not known in four cases, and excluding these the mean time on probation was 2.1 years (S.D. 1.21). As well as the custodial forms of care and probation, 153 boys (45.5 per cent of all offenders) paid fines, forty-seven (14.0 per cent) were given a conditional discharge, one was placed in the care of a local authority, thirty-five (10.4 per cent) were cautioned and ten (3.0 per cent) were given an absolute discharge.

CONCLUSIONS

Delinquency was associated with social class, and as expected there was an excess of delinquents from manual, but not agricultural, families. This measure of class was the socioeconomic group of the father when the Survey child was aged 15 years. However, a measure was also devised that took into account not only the father's occupation but also the social class of the parents' original families and the parents' achieved level of education, and this more comprehensive measure of social position, which is stable over time, is now used throughout and referred to as social group. It is associated rather differently with delinquency, when only the population of delinquents is considered, with the class bias concentrated in the anticipated direction in SAC scale scores 3 and 4 but not in the first two points on the scale. Age at first offence and sentencing were also described, and like the findings on delinquency and social group they raise questions that are discussed in later chapters.

CHAPTER 4

Family Structure

INTRODUCTION

In the same way that we seem almost instinctively to look back in time for the explanation of certain kinds of behaviour — and arguably delinquency is one of them — so it seems to have been inevitable that studies of criminal behaviour should turn to the individual's family life in seeking an explanation. Mannheim (1965) said that

> for the normal family in a normal democratic Western society it is true to say that the child learns to behave socially not so much out of respect for the abstract, at best only theoretically understood, state code of conduct, but out of love for his parents, and if this latter incentive should not prove strong enough the other is almost certain to break down. Therefore, according to this view the whole, slow and often painful, process of the child's socialization depends on his early relationship to his parents. In an American investigation of the 'correlation between the moral judgements of children and their associates' it was found that these judgements were derived from those of the parents far more than from anybody else. [p. 609]

This chapter makes use of longitudinal data on home and family circumstances to look at many of the things that traditionally have been said to be associated with delinquency. The Western tradition of childhood sees it as a time when moral, intellectual and physical foundations are laid for many aspects of later life. Medical studies have shown associations between nutrition, physical environment and care in early life and later experience of disease, and social and psychological research has demonstrated links between emotional disruption in early life and some kinds of behaviour in later life. The importance of early life as a basis for adult character and

34

development is also part of our traditional 'knowledge'; most people believe that the child's upbringing in the first seven years has a profound and lasting effect on behaviour, morals and beliefs throughout adult life. When adults disapprove of adolescent behaviour they very commonly attribute it to poor upbringing (Banks *et al.*, 1975). Yet social and psychological research has not found universally damaging factors or events; many studies have found associations but cannot explain why some children have a potentially damaging experience and escape apparently unscathed. Since the present investigation has the advantage of information collected throughout the individual's life time, it is possible, for example, not only to look for associations and explanations of associations of, say, family size and delinquency, but to compare rates of family growth and to seek effects of different lengths of time as an only or perhaps youngest child. The aetiological 'usefulness' of the life history information is examined by seeing how well it discriminates delinquents from non-delinquents, and how many actual delinquents it wrongly identifies as non-delinquents and how many actual non-delinquents it wrongly identifies as delinquents. In other words it will be possible to say how far everyday impressions, for example that delinquents mainly come from disturbed family backgrounds or large families, are actually true, and then, in the concluding chapter, to examine what use may be made of such knowledge.

MATERNAL AGE AT MARRIAGE AND TIME MARRIED BEFORE THE FIRST BIRTH

Maternal age at marriage may be related to family size and delinquency for a number of reasons. First, most middle-class people experience their lowest earning capacity in their early years, and those who have children during this time may well have to bring them up in generally poorer circumstances than those who postpone the birth of their first child. Second, earlier marriages are usually in manual social-group families, more so before 1946, when these marriages occurred, than now. In this sample, 15.1 per cent of Survey member's mothers in non-manual families were married by age 20 years, as compared with almost twice the proportion (28.7 per cent) of manual group mothers. It has already been shown (in chapter 3) that manual social-group boys had a greater chance of delinquency than others. Third, there is an increased likelihood of divorce associated with early marriages, and divorce is itself associated with delinquency (see chapter 5 and the discussion in the concluding chapter). In a cohort of women married in 1951 the Office of Population Censuses and Surveys found that divorce rates among those married under age 20 years were twice as high per 1000 marriages as among those aged 20-24 years at marriage, whatever the marriage duration (Central Statistical Office, 1975). In this study, significantly more of the mothers who were married under age 20 years were divorced or separated when compared with those married after that age, but not more so among mothers of delinquents than others.

Maternal age may also affect the mother-child relationship. In their study of how 379 American mothers were bringing up their five-year-old children, Sears *et al.* (1957) felt that in Western society young motherhood

> imposes responsibilities too rapidly, requiring an emotional maturity the younger mother does not yet fully possess. Also, when children arrive so early, the parents usually have not been married long, and the young woman is forced to make her adjustments to marriage and motherhood simultaneously. In any case, it is strikingly clear that the older a mother was, the warmer she was towards her child, except when the child was a first one. [pp. 58-9]

It might also be argued that the longer the marriage before the first birth the greater the chance of good material home circumstances.

In this study, likelihood of indictable offending was significantly greater for boys whose mothers had married when they were aged under 20 (13.2 per cent delinquent) or over 30 years (10.5 per cent delinquent). For the younger mothers this association was statistically significant in the manual class and only when the husband was of the same or similar (+5 or −2 years) age. Nine of the eighty-six mothers married after age 30 years had sons who later committed indictable offences,. and five of these boys scored 3 or 4 on the SAC scale.

There was some evidence from those families where the Survey child was the first born that the longer the parents were married and without children the less the likelihood of later delinquency of a Survey child. Among Survey members who were first born those whose parents had been married for less than a year before this birth

(41), 14.6 per cent had committed at least one indictable offence by their twenty-first birthday; of those who were married for anything from one to three years before this first birth (450), 8.6 per cent had delinquent sons by age 21 years; and of those married for 4 or more years (310), 4.5 per cent had delinquent sons by this age.

Although illegitimate children were excluded from this study because of the original sampling decision, it was possible to look at delinquency rates among those first-born Survey members who were probably pre-marital conceptions; they were no greater than among those who were definitely not pre-marital conceptions.

FAMILY STRUCTURE

If, as seems so in this study, the amount of time parents spend with children is of some significance, then whether this is largely the result of the consequent emotional stability of the marriage as Sears, Maccoby and Levin (1957) suggest, or whether it is mainly because of improved economic circumstances, it is important to examine birth spacing of offspring who are later than first born, since this might well have a comparable effect. Close birth spacing will often reduce chances for the mother to contribute additional income, and diminish the time she can spend with the youngest child's brothers and sisters, and with her husband. There are, therefore, good reasons to investigate birth spacing, and it is considered now in three ways: first as birth order, next as family size and then as birth order in association with family growth.

Birth order

Like maternal age, birth order has often been shown to be associated with delinquency, and there is a long and chequered history of findings, itself of considerable relevance to the sociologist (Wadsworth, in preparation). The work originates in the medical investigations on criminals undertaken early this century by Goring (1919), who was himself much influenced by Pearson's statistical work on birth order. Pearson reported finding a greater prevalence of pulmonary tuberculosis and insanity in the first born. Goring refers to this and concludes of convicts that

It is difficult to see how environmental conditions, peculiar to a limited family circle, could play any part of importance in the incidence of any of these heritable pathological states; the special incidence of these states in the earlier born can only be due to the fact that taints of tuberculosis and insanity are inherited in greater intensity by older rather than by younger members of a family. We would, accordingly be inclined to attribute the increased tendency of elder members to be criminally convicted to their possessing, in some way, an increased intensity of constitutional criminal taint. [pp. 204-5]

Others after Goring came to similar conclusions, and in those early years such findings were used in support of hypotheses about heritability and crime. It is in the work of Adler (1932) that signs of recognition of the social context of the importance of birth order are to be found, together with discussion of its psychological significance. Adler pointed out that an advantageous status of the oldest child is traditional among many people and classes, and whilst agreeing with others that the first born was liable to 'a good deal of attention and spoiling', he noted that this was true of youngest children too. The unique feature of the first born is what Adler referred to as the experience of being ousted from his position, or 'dethroned', whereas the youngest child never has this experience. Adler claimed that experiences in early life laid the foundation for the individual's interpretation of his life in society thereafter. 'The main features of the criminal's personality have already been decided by the time he is four or five years old; by that time he has already made those mistakes in his estimate of himself and of the world which we see displayed in his criminal career' (p. 218). Criminals who were oldest children, for example, were those 'who felt very deeply the arrival of another child and their sense of deprivation had moulded their whole life style' (p. 144). Of recent years the tendency has been to see birth order in its social context, and to consider its effect on maternal attention. The McCords and Zola (1959) found greatest delinquency among middle children followed by the youngest; their explanation is the lack of a period as the only child and the increased chance of being an infant when 'burdens of the family are most pressing'. Nye (1958) felt that the oldest child was least delinquent in his investigation because 'the oldest child often plays a semi-adult role in that he exercises control over, and to some extent is responsible for, younger siblings. Successful performance of this role requires acceptance of adult behaviour patterns' (p. 37).

Unfortunately birth order has not always been clearly defined.

Fortes (1933) drew attention to the need for definition in the separation of his study population into the 'true-sib' group, where all family members were biologically related, and the 'step-sib' group where this was not so. Burt (1925) is one of the few researchers who referred to the importance of definition of these terms. However, he counted as only children all those who grew up more or less without siblings nearby in age, irrespective of their birth position, thus getting the worst both of what might have been a control for size of inter-sib interval, and of a real attempt to define only children. It was Miller (1944) who set out three possible definitions of birth order:

(a) Pregnancy order (including all still births and miscarriages)
(b) Birth order (comprising only live children)
(c) Fraternal position (those living in the surviving sibship at a specified time)

In this study, birth order comprises all biologically related siblings of the Survey member. Whilst the study population was aged from birth to 15 years only thirty-nine non-delinquents (2.1 per cent of all non-delinquents) lived in families with step, half, fostered or adopted sibs, as did eighteen delinquents (5.4 per cent of all delinquents). Not only do such small numbers preclude further analysis, but so too do the very different circumstances of each of these cases: some Survey members were born of parents who already had children from a previous marriage, some experienced the arrival of older or younger children of a step-parent, some experienced the birth of a new half sibling to a step-parent, and yet others went to live with foster parents or relations and acquired siblings through adoption. The greater percentage of delinquents having this experience is explained by their greater experience of broken homes (see chapter 5).

In this study, the chance of committing a delinquent act, whether an indictable offence or not, rose significantly with increasing birth order in all types of crime on the SAC scale, regardless of social group. In other words, first born children were least likely to be delinquent, and fourth and later born most likely.

The particular attention that has been given to the position of only children is understandable in the light of the findings in this study, as shown in Table 4.1. This position has been regarded as in some ways particularly vulnerable, being either more vulnerable to delinquency because of the dangers of 'spoiling' the child by excessive

TABLE 4.1 *Length of time as only child and delinquency*

Family position	No delinquency	Non-indictable offence(s)	One indictable offence	More than one indictable offence	Total (=100%)
	%	%	%	%	
Only child to age 11 years	91.1	3.3	4.8	0.7	270
Only child to age 6 years	92.2	2.1	5.0	0.7	141
Only child to age 4 years	90.2	1.7	6.0	2.1	234
Only child to age 2 years	86.7	3.0	6.7	3.7	270
Never an only child	81.1	6.2	8.3	4.4	1281

$X^2 = 39.85$ with 12 d.f. p < .001

parental attention, or less vulnerable to delinquency because of the sole maternal attention that goes with it. It is evident that in this study being an only child had a significantly protective effect against delinquency, whatever the length of time spent as an only child, although this effect was greatest in the first four years of life. Being an only child for longer than this, up to age 11 years, tended to reduce the chance of indictable offending and increase that of non-indictable offending, but these effects seem specific to certain types of crime. Offenders in each of the SAC scale categories were more commonly boys who had been only children for a relatively

TABLE 4.2 *The percentage of offenders among those who were only children for three years or more compared with all others, broken down by social group and social acceptability of crime scale score*

	Non-manual		Total non-manual boys in each group	Manual		Total manual boys in each group
	SAC scale scores			SAC scale scores		
	1 and 2	3 and 4		1 and 2	3 and 4	
Only child for 3 years or longer	6.4	1.2	342	7.0	3.6	302
Never an only child, or only child for 2 years or less	7.2	3.7	600	12.5	9.6	947

short time, or not at all, compared with those who had been only children for three years or longer (see Table 4.2). Among only children, offence rates are related in different ways to the length of time of sole maternal attention received. Rates of the socially most acceptable offences change hardly at all with changes in time spent as the only child, rising for those who were only children for longest. However, rates of the socially least acceptable crimes change considerably. Those scoring 3 show a drop in rate as the amount of maternal attention increases up to age 6 years, but a slight rise between 6 and 11 years. Those scoring 4, that is those who committed sexual or violent offences, show a drop in rate only up to 4 years, and practically no change thereafter.

Of course, more than half of the boys in the study population (58.3 per cent) had never been the only child of their parents. In comparison with others who at age 4 years were middle or youngest children in their families, the first born was still significantly less likely later to become delinquent. Chances of delinquency by middle or youngest children increased significantly with increasing numbers of children, particularly when there were four or more. That these relationships are only statistically significant for manual social-group children makes it possible that they reflect environmental factors such as overcrowding and poor home conditions, but even if this is so (and the arguments for this are examined later) they might still also reflect differential maternal attention.

Family size

West (1967) said that a 'point on which investigators all agree is that families with a large number of children contribute a disproportion-ately large number of juvenile delinquents' (p. 73), and he went on to point out that the link 'between size of family and other things shows once again how consideration of any one of these social background factors leads to all the rest' (p. 74). However, very few investigators have examined exactly what it is about large families that leads to this common agreement on their relationship with delinquency. Ferguson (1952), among the relatively few who attempt an ex-planation, concluded that the relationship was explained by over-crowding (p. 22), and West and Farrington (1973) also found overcrowding, together with low income, to be explanatory (p. 33).

Wootton (1959) has drawn attention to the association of poverty with large family size in her observation that

> . . . the parents of these large families are faced with quite exceptionally difficult problems, failure to cope adequately with which might well be a sign, not so much of their own sub-normality, as of their lack of the supra-normal qualities which the situation demands. Family allowances notwithstanding, the household with several young children dependent solely on parental earnings constitutes today one of the economically most hard pressed sections of our community; one man's wage is not enough, and the mother of a large family has too much to do at home to be able to supplement this effectively. It may thus well be true that problem families are the victims as much of their economic circumstances as of their own personal shortcomings, and that these shortcomings are themselves, at least in part, the reaction of despair to impossible demands. [p. 59]

That investigators have looked specifically to large family size in studies of delinquency may well have become accepted tradition since the eugenicist's view that the many children of problem families contribute to undesirable strains in the population in a disproportionate manner. Other explanations are now being put forward as discussed above. In his study Nye (1958) found that, 'for boys, delinquent behaviour is less in small families' and he concluded that 'difference in family size is probably more closely related to internal and indirect than to direct controls' (p. 38). More recently, in their study of normal growth and development of four-year-old children in Nottingham, the Newsons (1968) found 'the mother of a small family has more opportunity both to observe and to talk to any individual child in it' (p. 185). It might also be that family size effects are class biassed and that it is only large families in the manual social group that have such features as overcrowding that seem to be related to delinquency. Indeed the Newsons (1968) noted this in comparing mothers' reports of their own participation in play, as between social groups for different family sizes (pp. 172-3). A large family living in poor and overcrowded circumstances would certainly have a high likelihood of reduced maternal attention, possibly giving greater opportunities for children to be more often free from parental control.

In this study, family size is taken to be complete when Survey members were aged 15 years. Very few mothers were likely to have had further children after that time, since by then 95.4 per cent were aged 36 years or more. Mean assumed completed family size in this population was 3.04 children, and it was very significantly associated with delinquency. Whereas 9.1 per cent of families of only one child had delinquent sons, 10.1 per cent of those with two children had delinquent Survey member sons and 24.3 per cent of those with four or more had delinquent Survey member sons. This association was statistically significant only in the manual social group, but this should not be allowed to obscure the fact that 75.7 per cent of boys in large families did *not* become delinquent.

Empirical researchers seem not to have discussed the importance of 'visibility' of large families in contributing to the incidence of recidivism. 'Visibility' is used to mean that families with four or more children are more noticeable in the community simply by virtue of their size, and they are also usually either at one extreme or the other of the social-class spectrum. Once a boy from a large manual social-group family has committed his first offence he is more likely to be noticed and questioned if not at work, and to be regarded as a suspect. In the present study it was not possible to discover how much this sort of explanation accounted for the large jump from 2.2 per cent of boys in families of three becoming recidivist compared with 7.4 per cent in families of four or more, but it is likely to have made a contribution. Completed family size was also significantly associated with the SAC scale, and percentages of delinquents rose with increasing family size in each category of the scale.

In view of the association of both birth order and family size with delinquency the combination of these factors is now examined.

Birth spacing and family size

Families were divided into five groups of growth and birth spacing, and as table 4.3 shows over half of the male Survey population (57.4 per cent) had younger siblings. Not only was the existence of younger siblings associated with delinquency, but this association was more marked the later the family went on growing.

Did the existence of older sibs affect this relationship? Not only were first-born boys (i.e. those without older sibs) least likely to be delinquent, but within each type of family growth pattern those who had older sibs were more likely to be delinquent, and the more older sibs there were the greater the likelihood of delinquency. We have

TABLE 4.3   *The pattern of family growth and delinquency*

Family growth types and percentages in each type	No delinquency	Non-indictable offence(s)	Indictable offence(s)	Total (=100%)
No growth (42.6%)	88.0	5.0	7.0	817
EARLY ONLY - birth(s) whilst Survey member aged 0-4 years and none thereafter (22.1%)	86.6	4.5	8.9	424
INTERMEDIATE - birth(s) whilst Survey member aged 0-6 years and none thereafter (11.4%)	84.9	4.6	10.5	219
LATE ONLY - birth(s) only after Survey member aged 6 years (7.7%)	83.7	2.7	13.6	147
THROUGHOUT - births over the years while Survey member aged 0-15 years (16.1%)	78.3	4.9	16.8	309
TOTAL FAMILIES (1916=100%)				

$X^2 = 47.7$ with 12 d.f. $p < .001$

already seen that interruption of the period of *sole* maternal attention that first-born children enjoy was associated with an increased risk of later delinquency; it is also clear that those who were youngest children throughout their first fifteen years of life, and had therefore enjoyed some parental attention uninterrupted by the birth of subsequent siblings, also had a significantly lower chance of later becoming delinquent. The kinds of offences most affected by the birth of a later sib were those that scored 3 or 4 on the SAC scale. Among those who began life as youngest children but who then experienced the birth of a sibling (56.4 per cent of all second or subsequent born boys) there was no significant difference in likelihood of later delinquency whenever the next birth occurred.

The same questions arise now as in the case of birth order: that is, is this increase in delinquency associated with late and continuous family growth a result of the poor environmental circumstances of many families in the latter position; is it accounted for, to some extent, by the remarriage of those who had lost or become separated from their first spouse and who perhaps were starting a second family; or is it something to do with the disruption and change of mother-child relationships that inevitably occur at the birth of a new baby? Although a study devoted solely to this subject would give the only certain answers to these questions, it is nevertheless possible to examine some aspects of these questions by having a suitably drawn sample to include enough first borns and enough very late births separated from older sibs by ten years or so.

Three measures of home environment were used: an indication of crowding (expressed as the number of persons per room); an indication of whether the home was owned or rented from the local authority or private landlord; and a count of whether or not certain amenities were available, namely hot water, bathroom and exclusive use of the kitchen. As expected, the families who experienced no growth had the best environmental circumstances and those who experienced growth throughout the fifteen-year period had the worst circumstances. As in the work of Baldwin and Bottoms (1976), delinquents in this study were significantly more likely to live in rented accommodation, particularly local authority housing. However, even when the effect of these environmental factors was accounted for (in a multiple regression analysis), the significance of the association of late and continuous family growth with delinquency was maintained. It was also maintained regardless of the health visitors' assessments of maternal care and management of the Survey child that were made when he or she was aged 4 years, even though families that experienced continuous growth had the poorest ratings, and the 'no growth' families the best. It is reasonable to conclude, therefore, that there was something in the pattern of family growth *per se* that was independently related to delinquency and, as in the case of the relationship of birth order and family size with delinquency, this was hypothesised to be maternal attention and the stable maintenance of parent-child relationships.

How much do all the data so far considered help in differentiating delinquents from non-delinquents? A discriminant analysis showed that they were fairly good at differentiating those who had committed break-in crimes and anti-personal crimes (80.8 per cent of these two groups) but much less successful at correctly placing those who had committed crimes of damage to property and thefts not involving break-ins (54.5 per cent correct) and not especially good with non-delinquents (63.6 per cent correct).

Some might be tempted to argue that if contemporaneously collected information such as this can be so relatively successful at picking out the socially least acceptable offenders some direct use could be made of it in practice, but this would be wholly wrong. This analysis attempted only to distinguish all delinquents from all others — because total numbers in each of the sub-divisions of the sac scale were so small — and so in practice there would be no way of deciding in which category of the scale any individual is actually likely to finish. In any event, 36.4 per cent of boys who in fact did not become delinquents would be wrongly discriminated as future delinquents, and 32.3 per cent of future delinquents would be wrongly discriminated as not likely to become delinquents in the future. The real use of such information lies in the clues it gives about aetiology, that is about the relatively greater importance of family size and growth and of the individual's birth order in their association with some kinds of offences rather than others, regardless of the relationships between these things and other factors such as the home physical environment.

CHAPTER 5

Disruption of Family Life

Introduction

Wootton (1959) observed that 'of all the hypotheses as to the origins of maladjustment or delinquency, perhaps the most generally accepted is that which associated such failure with the broken home' (p.118). However, although this subject is almost universally referred to and discussed in studies of delinquency, it suffers from poor data presented to substantiate findings. This is partly because the data have usually been recalled, and as Yarrow *et al.* (1970) demonstrated, recollection of mother-child relationships is particularly liable to distortion. Thus, there are likely to be unquantifiable errors about the dates and types of broken homes when data are collected retrospectively. West (1969) found that in his study, which began when the index children were aged 8 years,

> some of the mothers were vague or casual in their recollections, and there was reason to believe that certain separations, for instance those due to a father's imprisonment, tended to be suppressed, and that other incidents tended to be forgotten, especially so perhaps by the duller mothers or the harassed mothers of large families ... Perfect coverage is clearly unobtainable by retrospective enquiry from mothers . . . Difficulty in obtaining information is often associated with family disturbance. [pp.61, 63]

For the same reasons, information about other events and about their relationship in time with the family break are also likely to be inaccurate and distorted. Because of this, any attempt to question whether hypothesised effects of broken homes may be the result of *later* events connected with a family break (e.g., a decline in housing standards, or downward social mobility), or are specifically the

47

result of the emotional trauma of the break itself, is likely to be unsuccessful.

There is also the further complication, as Shaw and McKay (1931) noted, that coming from a broken home may itself give rise to 'a greater likelihood of a boy . . . being brought to court' (p.283). Nye (1958) also noted this possibility and found in his study that the chances of committal to institutional care following a court appearance were 'twice as great' (p.48) for a child from a broken home as for a child from any other home background.

Delinquency research is, of course, not the only field where insensitivity of data and lack of accurate data about broken homes is to be found. As recently as 1961, Yarrow noted the need for psychological studies of maternal deprivation to be concerned with the difference between institutionalisation, separation, multiple mothering and 'studies on distortion in the maternal-child relationship, for example, rejection, overprotection, ambivalence, on which there are many clinical reports, but few research reports'. The more sensitive psychological studies, both clinical and research, of maternal deprivation have mostly been prospective studies indicating an adverse outcome in terms of later emotional behavioural problems, lack of affection, neuroticism and social response difficulties. Most of this work has, however, been concerned with short-term effects, particularly of institutionalisation, and has lacked sensitive comparison of home and family relationships with those of the institution. Nevertheless, many studies conclude, as Yarrow (1961) hypothesised, 'that a close relationship with a mother-figure preceding separation will be followed by more severe immediate reaction but will be ultimately more favourable than a poor antecedent relationship'. More recent evidence for such a conclusion has come from a study of this cohort (Douglas, 1975), where

> the indications . . . are that the risks of disturbed behaviour following early admission [to hospital] would be reduced or eliminated if children who are highly dependent on their mothers or known to be under stress at home or to be showing excessive rivalry with a sib were treated at home or had their hospital admission postponed.

Most importantly, much of the psychological work concludes that the numbers of children affected by the experience of broken homes or maternal deprivation are, in fact, surprisingly small. Spitz and Wolf (1946) found severe reactions to maternal separation in only

19 of their 123 infants studied, and of Robertson and Bowlby's (1952) 45 children studied 20 apparently showed at most 'acute fretting'. Of Lewis's (1954) 500 deprived children, among the 100 who were subjected to personal follow-up only three were found to have marked personality disorders, and twenty-two had difficulties in relationships. Bowlby *et al.* (1956) concluded that the outcome from maternal deprivation 'is immensely varied, and of those who are damaged, only a small minority developed those very serious disabilities of personality which first drew attention to the pathogenic nature of the experience'.

There is a notable similarity of findings between studies about both the frequency and the importance of family breaks and later delinquency, but there is, too, a similarity of poor definition of family breaks, particularly of the type of break and the child's age at the time of the break. This lack of detail has, of course, often been because of inevitable restrictions in how data could be collected. However, two areas of movement towards greater specificity may be identified. The first is the relationship of family break to the type of crime committed, although it has received surprisingly little attention. Weeks (1940) found broken homes more often related to sex offences and to 'incorrigibility' than to other types of crime. Nye (1958) found 'ungovernability' such as truancy, running away from home, expulsion from school, driving without a licence, drinking illegally and defying parents (p.45) also to be associated particularly with broken homes. The McCords and Zola (1959) found practically all types of crime to be related to insecurity at home or to a love-starved home. But most recently Sterne (1964) found little relationship between type of delinquency and experience of a broken home.

Greater specificity is also to be found in the study of parent-child relationships. This is not surprising in view of recent work on birth order and family size, Bowlby's work (1947, 1956, 1970) on the damaging effect of early maternal separation, and Stott's (1950) study of approved school boys. There has been more concern with poor parental care for and interest in the child than with simply checking on whether broken homes were significantly related to delinquency or not, and there has been some interest too in the child's rejection of the parent. Thus some attempts have been made to discover what it is about break-down or poor functioning of parent-child relationships that leads to their association with delinquency.

FINDINGS

In this study, family breaks are divided into temporary and permanent disruptions. The effects of temporary disruptions are sought among information about working mothers and about hospitalisation of the child and of the parent. Permanent disruptions are taken to be caused by the death of a parent or by a family break involving divorce or permanent separation.

Temporary disruptions

Hospitalisation

During the Survey member's first fifteen years of life 35.5 per cent of mothers had been in hospital and so had 27.7 per cent of fathers, and although there was greater delinquency amongst Survey members whose mothers had been in hospital for a month or more this was not statistically significant. Those whose fathers had been hospitalised were no more likely than others to be delinquent.

During the first fifteen years of life 48.3 per cent of these boys had themselves stayed in hospital at some time, and as Douglas (1975) has shown boys in this cohort who were admitted to hospital more than once or for more than one week during the first five years of life were more likely to have been delinquent up to age 17 years than boys who were not in hospital during this time. The effect of hospital admissions during this period was examined therefore in relation to the information which has since become available about delinquency up to age 21 years. Following the earlier work, this analysis was solely concerned with single hospital admissions during the first five years of life, since the interpretation of findings about the ninety boys who were admitted more than once was difficult because of small numbers. The 382 boys who were admitted to hospital on one occasion during this time had a significantly greater chance of becoming delinquent in later life when compared with boys not admitted to hospital, and this increased chance was distributed throughout all SAC scale scores. Almost equal proportions of boys from each social group had been admitted to hospitals (18.8 per cent of non-manual and 17.7 per cent of manual boys), and although those who were admitted before age 3 years were slightly more likely to become delinquent than those admitted between 3 and 5 years, this was not a significantly greater likelihood. Since there was a possibility that mothers rated by health visitors with a low score for maternal care and management might have had children who were more at risk of a hospital admission during these early years, and since this may also have been true of very closely spaced families, the influence of these factors was accounted for to see whether, after this, knowledge of single early hospital admissions still significantly discriminated delinquents from non-delinquents, and it still did so.

But why should this be? Perhaps the length of the hospital stay was particularly important, and indeed Douglas (1975) found this to be so. It could also be that children undergoing particularly disturbing experiences while in hospital were most likely later to become delinquent, especially since at this time (1946-51) children were admitted with unpleasant diseases like mastoiditis, and since procedures such as anaesthesia were much more frightening than they generally are today. However, Douglas (1975) found no relationship between delinquency and reasons for admission to hospital, or between delinquency and medical procedures and treatment, or between delinquency and later effects of illness, such as persisting physical disability. He saw the effect of early hospital admission in terms of an additional emotional experience for those already emotionally vulnerable. The effects of first taking into account pre-hospitalisation vulnerability and then seeing what effect remains attributable to the hospital admission itself were that knowledge of hospital admission added nothing to the discriminant power of the family disruption data.

Working mothers

There is considerable literature on delinquency and working mothers, almost all of it concerned with the effects of mothers working while the children were teenagers; for the most part there is insufficient detail about hours worked and arrangements made for the care of the children. Analysis has also been insufficient; for example, the Gluecks (1950) found that 47 per cent of mothers of delinquents worked and that only 33 per cent of mothers of non-delinquents did so, but they did not examine these findings separately for each social group (p.112). The confusion in this area has been summarised by Wootton (1959) who observed that 'the American studies generally, therefore, can only be said to show results at least as diverse and as inconclusive as their British counterparts' (p.116). West and Farrington (1973) more recently found

> . . . that boys whose mothers had a full-time job included, unexpectedly, a smaller percentage of delinquents . . . The reason for this may have been that mothers in full-time work tended to produce a higher family income and fewer children both of which were factors associated with absence of delinquency . . . The finding is in conformity with the results of the National Child Development Study (Davie *et al.*, 1972), which demonstrated at age 7 years that children of full-time working mothers showed no marked ill effects in terms of their attainment or adjustment in school. The factors of family size and social class far outweighed any effect that could be attributed to working mothers. [pp.27-8]

In this study we know that 1125 mothers (67.2 per cent of all mothers — 60.4 per cent non-manual and 72.6 per cent of manual group mothers) had worked at some time while Survey boys were aged 0-15 years. We also know that in early life, that is while boys were aged 0-6 years, the proportion of mothers working was 23.7 per cent (16.5 per cent of non-manual mothers and 29.3 per cent of manual social-group mothers). If mothers had worked during this time in the boy's life there were significantly greater proportions of delinquents with each increasing score on the SAC scale, but statistical significance was only just reached. It could be that this relationship of early working mothers with later delinquency of sons might be accounted for as much, if not more, by other features of families that were themselves significantly related to delinquency - for example, close birth spacing, low social group and poor home environment. Certainly, mothers who worked while the survey child was aged 0-6 years were more likely to be in families where considerable growth had occurred during these years and to be from families that were broken while the survey child was aged 0-4 years. The income sensitive factors of social group, permanent family break while the child was 0-4 years, close family spacing, crowdedness at home and lack of home amenities were used in a multiple regression analysis to see whether once their influence had been taken into account the information on mothers working still discriminated delinquents from non-delinquents. Once these things were allowed for then information on mothers working had no significant effect on the discrimination of delinquents from non-delinquents.

But we also have some more detailed information on a smaller number of mothers who worked while their children were aged 0-6 years, on 454 mothers of non-delinquents (24.4 per cent) and 112 mothers of delinquents (33.3 per cent). This information consists of hours worked, number of jobs held and the boy's exact age at the beginning and ending of each job. This information was compared as between delinquents and non-delinquents and no significant differences were found.

Permanent disruptions

By the time they were aged 15 years, 280 boys (12.8 per cent) had experienced a broken home, almost exactly the same percentage in the non-manual social group (12.3 per cent) as in the manual group (13.1 per cent). Almost a third of all breaks took place while the Survey member was aged 0-4 years, whatever the social group. Family breaks were more often the result of death in the manual social group (51.2 per cent) than in the non-manual group (45.7 per cent), and divorce or separation was thus slightly commoner in the non-manual group (54.3 per cent of breaks) than in the manual group (48.8 per cent). Deaths of Survey members' parents were mainly of fathers (seventy-seven fathers of non-delinquents and thirteen fathers of delinquents); only forty-seven boys (thirty-eight non-delinquents and nine delinquents) experienced the death of their mother.

Of all those families that were permanently broken, 34.0 per cent experienced remarriage by the time the Survey member was aged 15 years, with equal proportions of non-manual and manual groups having this experience. Divorce or separation was more often followed by remarriage (42.7 per cent) than was death (26.7 per cent). Remarriage was almost significantly related to an increase in likelihood of delinquency, but not to any particular time during the Survey member's life at which it occurred. The association of early family breaks (0-4 years) with later delinquency was not significantly changed by remarriage, but among breaks occurring whilst the Survey member was aged beteen 4 and 15 years remarriage had an increased chance of being followed by delinquency. The effect of the type of permanent family break on delinquency was modified by remarriage only if the break had been caused by the death of a parent; the effects of divorce and separation were not changed. Unfortunately numbers were too small for further analysis.

TABLE 5.1 *Social acceptability of crime scale and time of family break*

Age of Survey member at time of break	Social acceptability of crime scale					Total (=100%)
	0 No crime	1	2	3	4	
No break	85.8	2.4	6.6	3.5	1.6	1911
0-4 years	69.3	1.1	11.4	12.5	5.7	88
4-8 years	78.5	4.6	10.8	4.6	1.5	65
8-11 years	79.5	–	12.8	2.6	5.1	39
11-15 years	90.1	1.4	2.8	5.6	–	71
Unknown age	(13)	(0)	(2)	(2)	(0)	17

The fact of a family break was significantly related to delinquency, and Table 5.1 shows greatest differences were to be found when comparing families that were never broken with those broken when the Survey member was aged 0-4 years, and this significance holds good in both social groups. The type of break particularly associated with delinquency is shown in Table 5.2, where there is a clear

TABLE 5.2 *Social acceptability of crime scale and type of family break experienced*

Type of break	Social acceptability of crime scale					Total (=100%)
	0 No crime	1	2	3	4	
No break	85.8	2.4	6.6	3.5	1.6	1911
Death of father	85.6	2.2	8.9	1.1	2.2	90
Death of mother	80.9	2.1	6.4	8.5	2.1	47
Divorce or separation	73.4	1.4	10.5	11.2	3.5	143

distinction between breaks that were more likely to have happened suddenly, which seem to be very little different in effect from no breaks, and breaks that could 'be seen to be coming', which were associated with considerably higher incidences of delinquency. This is especially true of divorce or separation, and was statistically significant in both social groups. The earliest family breaks were particularly associated with the least acceptable offences (SAC scores 3 and 4); this, too, is a relationship that is statistically significant in both social groups. Most differences in incidence of crime types were associated with divorce or separation, rather than with death of parents.

The suggestion made both by Shaw and McKay (1931) and more recently by Nye (1958), that children from broken homes might be more likely than other children to experience more rigorous treatment at the hands of the law, is confirmed by the present findings. Boys from homes broken by divorce or separation were much more likely than boys from other kinds of homes to suffer custodial treatment, and this was particularly true for boys who had lived through a family break while they were aged 0-4 years; this was the case even within SAC scale types. As far as the small numbers permit these relationships are found within both the non-manual and the manual groups.

DISCUSSION

So far National Survey findings are in agreement with the general kind of conclusions of other studies. There is evident association of delinquency and broken homes; it is particularly associated with disruptions from normal family functioning, as for example the McCords and Zola (1959) and Nye (1958) also found; it is especially associated with breaks that occurred when boys were in their first four years of life, as the psychological studies suggest; it does predispose offenders to custodial care rather than the non-custodial forms of treatment, and it is not likely to account for a very large number of delinquents, as Bowlby *et al.* (1956) suggested. Indeed, of all the 336 delinquents only sixty (17.9 per cent) had ever experienced a permanently broken home by the time they were aged 15 years, and similarly only 11.8 per cent of non-delinquents also had this experience.

Two effects may be hypothesised to account for this relationship between delinquency and broken homes. It may be that the immediate and emotional circumstances of the break itself are the most important features of this relationship, or alternatively it may be that family breaks are associated with changes in families' social circumstances which are, in turn, related to delinquency.

Any hypothesis that sought an explanation for these present

findings in the emotional stress of the family break itself might be expected to be on particularly firm ground. It is the only hypothesis that most researchers have used, and there have been some persuasive arguments in its favour from a very wide range of psychological studies. Rutter (1966) has noted that chronic physical illness in a parent that leads to death was often a source of psychiatric disturbance in children, and Bowlby and Parkes (1970) and Marris (1958) have pointed out the important effect of the grief reaction of the surviving parent. That delinquency in this study was particularly related to divorce and separation when it occurred during the index child's first four years of life also supports this hypothesis. This type of break is, more than any other, likely to take place in an atmosphere of quarrelling, discord and emotional upheaval, it is likely to be more difficult than death to explain to a child under age 5 years, and the emotional upheaval associated with it will usually continue for longer than in any other type of break. Few have been able to examine the possible supportive role of grandparents and of siblings in the circumstances of an early family break, but these could help to account for the fact that not all children of broken homes are similarly affected.

Relatively little attention has been given to the possibility that loss of income and subsequent changes in the broken families' fortunes could be hypothesised to be the explanation for their relationship with delinquency. Even without the loss in income that most broken families suffer, at least temporarily, and certainly with it, the social life of both the children and the remaining parent will change. For the child this could mean an apparent reduction of interest in school work and concentration at school. Also some families will have to move, possibly to shared accommodation with parents or others, and some families will be obliged to move into humbler homes. Such changes in social life might well be important in the genesis of delinquency. Other later effects are the loss of a particular role model, as the Gluecks (1950) and others have suggested, possible changes in the relationship between the remaining parent and children, the effect of the step-parent, and the possible importance of the role model of the family as disturbed.

It is therefore necessary to see whether the relationship between delinquency and homes permanently broken during the first four years of a child's life may be explained by the late effects of the experience of a broken home rather than by the emotional disturbance of the circumstances of the break itself. Late effects were sought in data on home physical circumstances, in teacher - parent relationships, in health visitor's assessments of the maternal care of this child and in the family structure following the break.

There is no doubt that broken families suffered a decline in home circumstances. Both non-manual and manual broken families significantly more often lacked certain basic home amenities exclusive use of a kitchen, availability of a bathroom and of a hot water supply when compared with families that were not broken, and children in manual families more often shared beds after a family break, particularly after divorce or separation; broken families were also significantly more crowded, in terms of persons per room. There was a much reduced chance of home ownership among those families who experienced a broken home, and this chance increased the longer the marriage had existed, possibly because of the correspondingly reduced chances of remarriage. These differences were accounted for by family breaks caused by divorce or separation, but homes broken by death were, in this respect, very little affected. Yet despite these adverse changes in home circumstances a multiple regression analysis demonstrated that they did not account for the association between delinquency and life in a broken home.

In this study, teachers rated Survey boys' attitudes to work at age 10 years on a four-point scale (see Appendix). Schools were asked to ensure that whenever possible ratings were made by the teacher who knew the child best, preferably the child's current class teacher. At this time (1956) class teachers of children of this age were almost always sole teachers of their class. It should also be remembered that assessments made for the National Survey were in one important respect unlike those made for many other studies, in that the teacher was asked only to rate the Survey child, and not as is usually the case, all the children in the class, and so the commonly observed 'central tendency' of ratings was not a problem.

The usefulness of teachers' assessments needs to be made very clear. These ratings cannot be seen as 'objective measurements' of the child's behaviour, since other teachers would certainly make different ratings of the same child. These assessments should be interpreted as an indication of the child's relationship with the teacher making the assessment. Class teachers who report a child of age 10 years as 'lazy' are unlikely to behave towards this child in the same way as they would if he was thought to be 'attentive'.

Whatever the family's social class, teachers significantly more

often rated parents of boys from families already broken by divorce
or separation as less interested than others (from unbroken families)
in their son's progress at primary school. They also significantly
more often rated these boys as average or poor or lazy workers.
However, although adverse teachers' assessments were related to an
increased chance of a later delinquency, and although they were
significantly more likely for boys from broken homes, even when
these effects were accounted for by multivariate statistical techniques
the fact of living in a home that was broken in the first four years of
life still made an independent contribution to the discrimination of
delinquents from non-delinquents.

During the children's pre-school years health visitors (community
nurses) assessed the mother's management and understanding of the
child, her use of infant welfare and immunisation and vaccination
services, and the cleanliness and state of repair of the child's clothes
and shoes and of the home. Non-manual families that were broken
by divorce or separation before the Survey child was aged 5 years
were more often rated as dirtier than others and their mothers were
more often said to be worse at the management and understanding
of the child, less likely to use the infant welfare services and less
willing to take the health visitor's advice when compared with
others. Families broken by death were not distinguishable on these
ratings from unbroken families. These findings are particularly
difficult to interpret. They could indicate that the standards of home
care really do fall during and after family breaks by divorce or
separation, or they could be taken to mean that poor home care itself
predisposes a family break by divorce or separation; or again they
could be interpreted simply as an indication of bias by health visitors
in their assessment of care in these sorts of families. Home standards
really did drop, but the importance of poor home care as a
predisposing agent was impossible to assess with complete accuracy,
since these assessments were made when Survey children were aged
4 years, when most of the early breaks had already occurred.
However, since divorce or separation were a little more common
amongst non-manual families, and since more non-manual than
manual families experienced breaks during the index child's pre-
school years, it may be that *by comparison* with other non-manual
families those suffering divorce or separation really did seem to
have lower standards of home and maternal care. On the other hand,
there is some support for the interpretation of findings as being to an
extent, the result of observer bias, in that the health visitor

assessments of homes that were in fact to be broken later in the life of the child (i.e. after age 5 years) were at this time in no way different from their assessments of homes that were never broken. However, whatever the interpretations, statistical analysis showed that even allowing for the effects of these factors the family break information still contributed significantly to the discrimination of delinquents from non-delinquents. In other words, boys from broken homes had a greater chance than others of later becoming delinquents, but this was not simply because of the poor maternal care and management that health visitors reported to be a feature of their homes.

The importance for delinquency in boys of experiencing a broken home in early life seems incontestable in the face of the information about the social consequences of being from a broken home, although they are very real and very important. It is therefore necessary to look carefully at what information we have on the emotional effect of a family break at this age, and this will be done in chapter 9 (personality, behaviour assessments and physical development) and in the concluding chapter.

But apart from the problems of explaining how and why the association of broken homes and delinquency operates there still remains the aetiological question of whether knowing about a family break improves our chances of discriminating delinquents from non-delinquents. When this information was added to that on home and family circumstances it certainly improved on previous attempts to discriminate, but as Table 5.3 indicates even with this information 44 per cent of actual non-delinquents would still be wrongly predicted to be delinquents and 27 per cent of delinquents would be

TABLE 5.3 *Discrimination of delinquents and non-delinquents* *

	Non-delinquents	Social acceptability of crime scale			All delinquents
		2	3	4	
Correctly discriminated	56.3	66.3	76.2	87.1	73.1
Incorrectly discriminated	43.7	33.7	23.8	12.9	26.9
TOTAL (=100%)	1626	92	63	31	186

* Using data on birth order, family size, social group and family breaks caused by divorce, separation, death or prolonged absence of a parent, but omitting information on home physical environment and maternal care and management assessments.

wrongly predicted as non-delinquents, even though the discrimination of some kinds of delinquents was much better than others.

CHAPTER 6

Primary School

INTRODUCTION

When compulsory school begins at age 5 years this is the first time that all children are certain to be on their own in a social setting, supported by whatever experiences and resources they already have. They will go to school equipped with every kind of preparation specifically about school. From my own study of parental behaviour of Survey members it is evident that preparation for school is seen as anything from toilet training and doing up buttons, to academic and social preparation. The Newsons (1968) stress how most mothers know that 'it is important for the child to begin to learn something about the give and take of social life beyond the nucleus of his immediate family. In particular, the potential battleground of school looms ahead in the mother's mind' (p. 105). As school age approaches mothers begin to 'fear that they have already left it [independence training] too late' (p. 83), and wonder 'will he let me down?' (p. 313). Many mothers, of course, look forward to this as a period when they can have a little more time to themselves, or even return to work.

The academic literature on this subject is predominantly gloomy and it seems to be a miracle that so many children escape apparently unscathed. Wolff (1969) observed that 'the personality characteristics of children reared by the more punitive lower working class parents are such that they tend to react to the frustrations of educational failure with aggressive, antisocial behaviour and this in turn earns them further disapproval from their teachers. School life for such children is frustrating and engenders feelings of apathy in relation to work and achievement' (p. 147). It is important to ask whether so much can be laid at the door of such an indefinite concept as 'educational failure', especially since there is plenty of evidence that such failure is rooted in a complex of interacting home and school factors. In an earlier study of this cohort, for example, Douglas (1964) reported 'that between 8 and 11 years the deficiencies of parents are being offset by good teaching in the best primary schools, whereas in the worst schools even the children who are encouraged in their work by their parents have no advantage. By improving the level of teaching in the primary schools it seems that the waste of ability through lack of interest and stimulation at home can be much reduced and perhaps eliminated' (p. 110). At the beginning of the child's infant or even nursery school life, before an aura of educational success or failure has had an opportunity to be established, there may be a low level of rapport between the child and 'the school'. Bernstein (1973) noted that 'one child through his socialisation is already sensitive to the symbolic orders of the school whereas the second child is much less sensitive to the universalistic orders of the school. . . . It is also the case that school is also implicitly and explicitly transmitting values and their attendant morality which affect educational context and the context of education' (pp. 221-2). Through friendship with other children, through his relationships with the teacher and through parental interest and involvement (or reinforcement) in school matters a child is prepared for success or failure, for the school provides 'an important means by which the middle class child enhances his self respect, and this is not so for the working class child. His self respect is in fact more often damaged' (p. 58). Whilst not necessarily agreeing with Bernstein's views of the idea of class differences, the importance of something like self-respect with a positive *social* self-image seems clear, as does the role of home and school factors in its establishment.

It is important to remember that the process of coping with the social world of school involves not only the child's reactions to others, how he 'gets on' with others and the image he presents to others, but also the way he handles the reactions of others to him. This may be particularly stressful since at home and generally in the time before going to school strangers will have been presented to the child as friends of his parents, whereas in the new school situation strangers often have no 'prior image' for the child. How he handles their reaction to him is crucial in the establishment of the relationship. A child who the teacher has difficulty in hearing in the class, for example, will be asked — not necessarily roughly or strictly — to speak up, and if he does not do so the teacher will begin to think of him as a shy, quiet child and begin to treat him as a shy and quiet child. This sort of feedback process will occur in all areas of communication, and will be added to the teacher's other impressions of the child, impressions gained from his appearance, from his behaviour in the playground with other children, from meeting his mother and from seeing her in association with other mothers. The early school years must also be seen, therefore, as the first opportunity for consistent labelling of the child by strangers, and the first opportunity for him to be obliged to handle the effects of labelling.

To an extent these things may be examined by way of National Survey data. Although suffering the handicap of having no comments from the children themselves, the data do include the views of the teachers on each child's work and work involvement and on parental interest in the child's education. Also available are parents' own views of their active interest in the education of their child, as well as the information on home physical environment, family structure and changes and the physical development of the child. This chapter examines the relationship of these things with delinquency, and assesses how much they contribute to what has already been achieved by earlier data in the discrimination of delinquents from non-delinquents.

THE PRIMARY SCHOOL AND ITS SOCIAL SETTING

Although there were very few differences in rates of later delinquency as between types of primary school, whether they were urban or rural, large (over 400 pupils) or small (under 100 pupils), nevertheless urban primary school boys had a tendency more often to grow up to be recidivists. Those in schools in poor physical circumstances also had a slightly greater likelihood of being classified as an offender while aged between 8 and 11 years. The predominant social class of the majority of pupils at the school seemed to have little association with delinquency. The only really significant effect of this aspect of primary school was to be found in its usual success rate for pupils in the examinations for entry to selective schools at age 11 years. Boys at primary schools with relatively low success rates had a significantly greater chance of becoming delinquent. The importance of the school's success rate remained, even in the case of boys who were notably greater achievers on certain educational tests (described later) than their school fellows.

The boy in the classroom

There was no association of delinquency with mixed or single sex primary schools. Although the teacher/pupil ratio seemed also to be of little importance, there were differences in this respect between urban and rural schools. Despite the inconclusive evidence — inconclusive because of small numbers and the insensitivity of the teacher/pupil ratio as a measure of what actually happens in a classroom — it was clear that in both rural and urban schools the fewer pupils for each full-time teacher the smaller the proportion of delinquent children. Could it be that where schools had small teacher/pupil ratios (i.e., when there were relatively few pupils to each teacher) and the teachers knew pupils well, when a *possible* prosecution was discussed — i.e., following a detection — then *actual* prosecution was less likely to follow than for pupils who were less well known to the teacher and who would have a correspondingly reduced chance of someone to intercede on their behalf? This was difficult to ascertain from these data for boys in rural schools because of relatively small numbers. Certainly there were no statistically significant differences between proportions of delinquents in each social group within teacher/pupil ratio bands. In urban schools, social-group differences were significant only when there was one teacher for thirty or more pupils, which was true for the majority (77.5 per cent) of urban Survey members.

TABLE 6.1   *Class teachers' assessments of boys' attitudes to work at age 10 years and later delinquency.*

Teacher's assessment	No offences	Non-indictable offence(s)	One or more indictable offences	Total (=100%)
Very hard or hard worker	91.2	3.5	5.3	656
Average worker	85.2	5.3	9.5	812
Poor or lazy worker	79.4	4.5	16.1	330

$x^2 = 33.85$ with 4 d.f. $p < .001$

As already mentioned in the previous chapter, primary school teachers rated each child's attitude to work at age 10 years, and as

Table 6.1 shows this was significantly associated with later delinquency even when, as in this table, the boys already known to be
delinquent are omitted. This association was statistically significant
only in the manual social class. Should we interpret this as meaning
that by their classroom behaviour future delinquent boys really
were distinguishable from others, or were boys who were already
known to the teacher to come from a poor home background or from
a broken home or who were low achievers therefore much more
likely to be rated as poor or lazy workers? If teachers were more
inclined to give poor ratings to boys from particular kinds of home
background, our knowledge of this rating might add very little to
the discriminatory power of other information of this kind. It might
also be an example of a self-fulfilling prophecy in the sense that
perhaps boys who had already acquired an attribute commonly
'known' to be connected with delinquency by the time this rating was
made — e.g. having divorced or separated parents — would have an
increased chance of being labelled with this other 'known' pre-
delinquent kind of behaviour. Both boys and girls who were rated as
poor or lazy workers were indeed also significantly more likely to
have come from homes already broken by divorce or separation,
and boys were also more likely to be of lower social class, higher
birth order and from a large family and to have parents with the
minimum of education who were rated by teachers as having little
interest in the progress of their child at primary school. There was
some evidence to support the view that teachers may have more
readily given a poorer rating to boys from families already broken
by divorce or separation, in that not only was this a statistically
significant association but also teachers did not significantly distinguish boys from homes that would in future (by the time they were
aged 15 years) be broken in this way. The relationship of this
assessment with parental interest and with birth order and family
size remains significant in both non-manual and manual social
groups, but the relationship with family breaks (up to age 10 years)
and with parental education was significant only in the non-manual
social group. The latter may be because of the small range of
educational differences among manual-class fathers, of whom only
fifty-two (6.0 per cent) achieved more than the most basic educational
level.

If we omit boys with attributes that we already know to be good
discriminators of delinquency as well as those with factors that tend

to predispose teachers to make adverse assessments, do teachers' assessments still relate to later delinquency? Certainly within the sub-population of boys from homes that were not broken by this age, boys who were only children at some time up to their fourth birthday and boys whose mother's care and management were assessed as average or high, delinquency was significantly related to poor scoring on the teacher's assessment at the p< .01 level or better. It does therefore seem that the teacher's assessment had some discriminatory value in its own right. This was further examined in a stepwise multiple regression analysis to test the independence of this variable when family circumstances already shown to be associated with delinquency were first taken into account. Even when all those data were accounted for, the teacher's assessment still contributed significantly to the discrimination of delinquents from non-delinquents.

TEST SCORES

At age 8 years all Survey members who were at school took four tests, of non-verbal intelligence, reading comprehension, mechanical word reading and vocabulary (see Appendix for detailed descriptions of tests). Any kind of offending was associated with an aggregate score that was significantly lower than the mean aggregate score for non-offenders, and the significance of these differences increased as delinquency became more frequent and as SAC scale score rose. Exactly the same results were found when each of the four tests was considered separately.

All these scores, however, also declined steadily and significantly with each downward step of social group and birth order. Mean aggregate scores of children who were not first born were significantly lower than those of first born children, and those of children who were first born but only children for less than two years were just significantly lower than those of other first born who were only children for longer than two years. Even the non-verbal scores showed a significant difference as between first born and all others at this age.

Since the delinquents were much more likely to be later born boys from lower social-group families, these factors were controlled for, and the findings re-examined. Regression analysis showed that once the effects of social group and birth order had been taken into account then, even without considering the effects of teacher's ratings (which were, of course, also related to test scores), the aggregate score no longer made a significant contribution to the discrimination of delinquents from non-delinquents.

In *The Home and the School*, Douglas (1964) observed that 'as the effects of family size on test performance are just as great at eight years as at eleven, it seems that these deficiencies, if they do account for part of the poor performance of these children, take their effect in early life' (p. 99). It was not, therefore, surprising to find that at 11 years test scores (verbal and non-verbal intelligence, reading, arithmetic, vocabulary, and their aggregate score — details are given in the Appendix) were again all significantly lower for delinquents than for non-delinquents, and lower for recidivists than for other delinquents. But once social group and birth order were taken into account these scores made no significant contribution to understanding the difference between offenders and non-offenders.

Clearly, although these test scores were in part a measure of innate ability, they inevitably each contained an element of acquired ability (even the non-verbal intelligence tests). This element can be examined by looking at differences in test scores between ages 8 and 11 years and asking whether delinquents do as well as would be expected, given their social group and birth order. Under-achievement was particularly a feature of recidivists and of boys scoring 3 on the SAC scale, that is boys who committed offences of breaking and entering and large-scale theft and robbery. Boys who committed sexual or violent offences against other persons scored significantly less well than expected only on the test of non-verbal intelligence.

This investigation is not alone in finding that measures of 'intelligence' are not helpful discriminators of delinquents from non-delinquents, once adequate account has been taken of other factors (see e.g. McCord *et al.*, 1959). It does not, however, concur with the work of Marcus (1956) who found, in prison populations, that sexual and violent offenders scored less well on intelligence tests than thieves. In this study, although sexual and violent offenders (SAC scale score 4) did score significantly lower than non-offenders, there were no significant differences for any of the tests at 8 years or at 11 years between SAC scale 3 and 4 scorers. Indeed, in terms of the achievement measure, arrived at by looking at differences between observed and expected scores on 11-year tests, and allowing for social group and birth order, mean observed scores for sexual and violent offenders were significantly nearer to their expected mean than were the means of observed scores for boys placed at the third point on the SAC scale. This is not surprising in view of the social-class distribution of each of these groups of offenders. Differences between these findings and those of Marcus are most likely to be accounted for by the effect of sentencing policy on his sample, and the fact that sexual offenders in the National Survey were likely to be rather different from those in the Wakefield Prison study in view of the difference in age.

Like West (1969), the present study found that 'apparently intelligence and scholastic ability did nothing to protect the better class boy from developing behaviour problems' (p. 113). And eight-year-old boys in this study with test scores in the top quartile were equally likely to become delinquent whether they were in a predominantly manual or predominantly non-manual primary school.

RELATIONS BETWEEN THE HOME AND THE SCHOOL

Teachers' assessments of parental interest

A score of parental interest in each boy's primary school education was compiled from teachers' ratings of parents' interest in the child's school progress, teachers' reports of whether they had discussed the child's progress with parents during the previous year and the mother's reports of her frequency of contact with the child's primary school teacher. These were all asked when children were aged 10 to 11 years.

Like the teacher's assessment of the child's attitude to work in primary schools, the rating of parental interest was very significantly associated with delinquency (see Table 6.2); the lower the rating the greater the likelihood of later delinquency. This relationship was statistically significant within the two social groups, and remained so even when boys who committed no offences were compared with those who first offended during the secondary school years or later, i.e. some time after this assessment was made. Even boys in the lowest quartile of achievers, on the aggregate test scores at age 8 years, had a significantly reduced chance of later delinquency if their parents' interest in their education was highly rated, and boys

TABLE 6.2   *Teachers' ratings of parental interest in boys' primary school education, and delinquency*

Parental interest rating in quartiles	No offences	Non-indictable offence(s)	One indictable offence	More than one indictable offence	Total (=100%)
Lowest	75.0	6.6	11.3	7.0	529
Second	84.9	5.3	7.3	2.5	437
Third	89.2	4.5	4.7	1.7	424
Highest	92.5	2.3	4.0	1.3	478

$\chi^2 = 76.71$ with 9 d.f. $p < .001$

who were in the top quartile of scorers had a significantly increased chance of later delinquency if their parents' interest in education was rated as low.

As might be expected the teacher's rating was not independent of other factors. Mean aggregate test scores rose very significantly with rising teachers' ratings, so that whereas the mean aggregate test score for boys of parents rated in the lowest quartile of interest was 45.86 that for boys in the highest quartile was 56.15. These differences remained statistically significant within social groups.

The chances of parents scoring highly on this rating also depended on the teacher's rating of the child's attitude to work at primary school. Boys who were seen to be poor or lazy workers were very likely to have parents rated very low for interest in their primary school education, and so were boys whose mothers had the minimum of formal education. Other factors that were less likely to be known to teachers were also related: there was a greater likelihood of low parental interest as birth order increased; low interest was also related to a poor maternal care and management score, and to being in a family broken by parental divorce or separation by the time this child was aged 5 years. There was some evidence of teachers' bias, in that they significantly more often rated both boys and girls from homes broken by divorce or separation by their fifth birthday with low parental interest scores, but failed to distinguish those whose homes were to be broken by the time they were fifteen but that had not yet become so. All of these relationships remained significant in both social groups.

Although there was no way of actually knowing how far, or indeed if at all, teachers were biased in making these ratings by their knowledge of the parents and of the child's home background, and how far these differences reflected a 'real' relative lack of parental interest in the primary school education of those in deprived circumstances, it was possible to investigate whether the teachers' rating of parental interest was still a discriminator of delinquency when all these other factors were taken into consideration.

Both of the variables that have been shown to be related to parental interest (teachers' assessments of work attitude and of parental interest) were used in a regression analysis to see how much each contributed to the discrimination of delinquents from non-delinquents once the effects of social group and family size and structure, including details of family breaks, were accounted for. Once this analysis had been carried out both measures still contributed very significantly to the discrimination at the $p < .001$ level. Evidently this measure of parental interest was a powerful explanatory variable even when the effect of these other variables and social group was taken into account.

Absence from school

Absence from school was significantly associated with delinquency only if it was the result of accidental injury (we have no information on non-accidental injury), and this was so in both social groups.

There is plenty of evidence from aviation medicine and from industrial psychology (see e.g. Haddon *et al.*, 1964) to indicate that in adults accidents are often associated with some kind of emotional upset or disruption of social life. It therefore seemed worthwhile to look for explanations in these kinds of data, especially since significantly more of the boys whose parents were rated as least interested had school absences of two or more weeks because of accidental injury.

However, once account was taken of the effect on the discrimination of delinquents from non-delinquents of social group, family break experience, family size and structure, parental interest in education and the assessments of maternal care, then absence because of accidental injury no longer made a significant contribution to the discrimination.

Job wishes of parents for boys

When boys were aged 11 years school nurses asked their mothers what sort of jobs they wanted their sons to do. Job wishes were significantly associated with delinquency, and also with the SAC scale. As job aspirations fell from professional and other non-manual categories to manual and agricultural work, so delinquency rates rose, but this did not reach statistical significance in either social class. The trend was clearly in the expected direction only in the case of sons of manual workers, and for this group the proportion of boys becoming delinquent was halved when mothers aspired for their sons to have non-manual jobs.

Job wishes of mothers for their children were, of course, also closely related to other indicators of parental desire for their child to 'get on'. The lower the mother's own educational level, the lower the aspirations for her son's job. Similarly when parental interest in primary school progress was rated as low so were job aspirations, but then only statistically significantly so in manual-group families; lack of significance in the non-manual families may well be because 70 per cent of parents in this group were rated by teachers as being in the top two quintiles of parental interest in primary school education. Job wishes were similarly significantly related to social group and to birth order: increasing birth order brought lower job aspirations, and this was statistically significant in both manual and non-manual group families. Once the effect of these associated factors was taken into account the importance of parental job wish was then found to be of no significance.

Age at which mothers wanted their sons to leave school

In interviews with the school nurse when boys were age 11 years, mothers were asked about their son's expected school leaving date. The earlier the anticipated age of leaving school, the greater the likelihood of delinquency in both social groups.

Like the parental job wish for boys, expected age of leaving school was strongly related to parental interest in the child's school progress. Parents rated as having the greatest interest in their child's school progress wanted their sons to stay on longer at school, regardless of social class, and better educated mothers of both social groups wanted their sons to stay on at school for longer than did mothers with the minimum of education. Like parental job wish, anticipated school leaving age was oldest for first born boys and decreased with decreasing birth order; this, too, was statistically very significant for both social groups.

Evidently this variable is closely related to parental education and to the parents' present social class, and to class-related features of the child's primary school. It was therefore not surprising that despite its significant relationship with delinquency it contributed very little to explaining the discrimination of delinquents from non-delinquents. In a regression analysis, once parental social group and the Survey member's birth rank had been taken into account, the contribution made by anticipated age of leaving school was of no significance.

DISCUSSION

This chapter has looked at information on the children's experience of primary school, and it has shown that the factors most strongly related to delinquency were those with the greatest human element. That is to say that there was little or no importance attached to the type and size of school or its amenities, and the apparent relationship of test scores with delinquency was explained by differences in social group and birth order, although delinquents were found to be under-achievers in terms of expected test scores at age 11 years. This has been taken to indicate an environmental rather than an innate difference. Of apparently greater importance was the school's usual level of results in the 11+ examinations, in that if results were usually poor then delinquency was more likely than if the school usually had good results; this was the case whether the boy was of high or low measured ability. The predominant social-class structure of the school was also relevant; when boys were not of the predominant class they were slightly less likely to be delinquent, whether they were themselves from manual or non-manual social-group families. Teacher/pupil ratios were also found to be important. The fewer the pupils for each teacher the less the likelihood of later delinquency, and in urban primary schools significant social-group differences in proportions of those who were delinquent were found only when there were more than thirty pupils for each teacher in the school.

The importance of evidence of teachers' relationships with the children was also found in their assessments of the boys' attitudes to work. Boys who were said to be poor or lazy workers were very significantly more likely to become delinquent; however, this was predominantly true of manual social-group boys and of those from backgrounds generally considered to constitute an unfavourable prognosis for school progress and achievement, and indeed for delinquency. Although teachers' assessments were related to delinquency even after allowing for the effect of these intervening background factors, the question still remains as to how far these assessments might have been instrumental in the 'production' of later delinquency. If such assessments, which are after all by no means an 'objective measure', are known, as they must be, to other teachers in the school, and are passed on to secondary school teachers when the child is 11 years old, this sort of rating could well contain an element of self-fulfilling prophecy. It might also be that in the event of a possible prosecution an adverse teacher's report would tip the scale in favour of pursuance of the prosecution, rather than otherwise.

These two last observations about the teachers' ratings of the boys' attitudes to work also apply to the indicator of parental interest in the child's primary school progress, an indicator compiled both from teachers' records and assessments and from parental reports, which was also very significantly related to delinquency. It, too, was related to other home factors, such as low parental education, but it was also shown to be effectively related to delinquency even when these factors have been taken into consideration. This was the most powerful factor of all the information considered in this chapter, and it goes along with the arguments about the importance of parental attention and the stability of home life. Information about school absences also supports this argument. Greater absence was associated with delinquency only if it was because of accidental injury, which has itself been shown in other studies to be associated with emotional disturbance and the disruption of normal social life. Unfortunately National Survey information about accidents is not yet available, but in due course a thorough investigation of this finding will be made.

Since the assessments of parental interest and of the boy's attitude to work were the only data in this chapter that continued to have a significant relationship with delinquency after other factors were considered, it seemed obvious that they should be included in a discriminant analysis to see how far they correctly discriminated delinquents from others. However, since, as has been shown, it was also necessary to account for the effect of the information on family life in assessing the discriminative power of these two factors, it seemed logical to consider them all together, and to ask how much the information from this chapter contributed to our knowledge from previous chapters. This analysis added nine more correctly discriminated delinquents, but conclusions about discriminative power may not safely be drawn because a complete set of data on primary school experience was not available for all those for whom we have information on family circumstances.

This discriminant analysis and the examination of the data in this chapter show that the assessments of parental interest and of the Survey members' attitudes to work were very closely linked with the home and family data considered in chapters 4 and 5, although, as has been shown here, they were significantly and independently related to delinquency. Their original contribution to the understanding of delinquency was greatest for offenders who committed violent or sexual crimes (scored 4 on the SAC scale) and least for those who scored 2, but the amount of information they added to what was already known from the home and family data was small.

How far the relationship of these teachers' ratings with home background factors was a reflection of different behaviour by people from different backgrounds, or how far it could be accounted for by teachers being more ready to assess children from manual social-group families, large families and broken families as poor or lazy workers etc., cannot be known. What is certain, however, is that at this time (1956-7) most teachers would have known of the work of Bowlby and of other studies of the adverse influence of poor maternal care and maternal deprivation. We know, too, that a relatively low expectation by the teacher of the performance and capabilities of some children and parents will not only have contained the seeds of a self-fulfilling prophecy for the child and the family, but will also have been passed on to other teachers both in the primary and in the secondary school.

CHAPTER 7

Health and Development, and Reports of 'Disturbance'

Introduction

This chapter considers relationships between delinquency and reports of disturbed behaviour, measurements of height, weight and shape, and information about the achievement of certain developmental milestones and about illness.

Developmental milestones

During the pre-school years some information was collected about each child's achievement of certain developmental milestones, and this study has considered data about age at first walking and talking and about breast-feeding. Although none of this developmental information was related to delinquency it should be noted that it was collected retrospectively when the Survey child was aged 2 years. This is quite a long time period for recollection, since not only did the great majority of children first walk and talk and were weaned during their first year of life, but by the time this child was aged 2 years some mothers also had a subsequent pregnancy and birth, which would add to the chances of faulty recollection.

Illness

Apart from the information on illness contained in data about hospital admissions and school absences, the incidence of chronic illness has also been examined to see whether it relates to delinquency. A chronic illness was defined as 'a physical, usually non-fatal condition which lasted longer than three months in a given year or necessitated a period of continuous hospitalization of more than one month. In addition, conditions were included only if they were of sufficient severity to interfere with the child's ordinary activities in some degree' (Pless and Douglas, 1971). When the *types* of illness were examined, rather than whether or not the child received hospital treatment for them, no differences were found in incidence rates between delinquents and others.

PHYSICAL CHARACTERISTICS

There are, of course, good precedents for looking at the physical characteristics, in terms of shapes and size and rates of growth, of delinquents and non-delinquents. The precedents fall into two main groups, leaving aside the early studies of such workers as Lombroso (1913) or Goring (1919).

First, there are the early studies of Sheldon (1949) that were concerned with somatotyping. This technique classified body shape into one of three types (endomorph, ectomorph and mesomorph), each of which was said to be associated with a particular type of temperament. The Gluecks found this to be associated with delinquency in a study using controls (1956); so did Gibbens (1963) in an investigation of a sample of borstal boys, and so have Cortes and Gatti (1972) who, like Gibbens, used an institutionalised criminal population.

The second precedent is also concerned with physical characteristics, but studies in this group do not regard links between personality and physical characteristics as *inherent.* Walker (1965) has pointed out that what Sheldon and the Gluecks saw as characteristic mesomorphic behaviour may be 'an example of natural selection . . . the mesomorph's physique is the best adapted of the somatotypes to the sort of things that juvenile delinquents do — assault other people, climb walls, run away from the police' (p. 47). Perhaps West's (1969) statistically non-significant finding that 'being heavily built was also related to being badly behaved' (p. 34) is also an example of this.

Given these precedents it is not unreasonable to look for differences in physical shape between delinquents and non-delinquents. It would also be reasonable because of a tendency already found for delinquents to have a rather different and poorer socialisation in very early life. If it was argued that some features of poor socialisation, such as being in a broken home, were related to emotional disruption, then there are medical reasons to expect some differences in shape, although improvements in emotional circumstances may result in a return to normal shape, or recovery of growth rate. Emotionally stunted children grow less well than others — the failure to thrive syndrome — and in adolescence emotional stress may be related to weight and shape changes, the extreme example being anorexia nervosa.

In the National Survey, heights and weights of children were obtained at special medical examinations held in school at ages 6, 7, 11 and 15 years. During the pre-school years, in addition to birth weight, heights and weights were taken by health visitors at Infant Welfare Clinics at ages 2 and 4 years. No somatotyping was attempted, but the information on the time of onset of puberty was collected, and this is discussed later. In examining the relationships of heights and weights at various ages with delinquency it was found that any significant difference occurred in the most socially unacceptable part of the SAC scale. Boys who scored 4 on this scale were significantly shorter than non-delinquents, and these same boys also tended to be lighter. Could these differences in fact be attributed to the social-class and birth order differences that have been shown to be associated with physical growth rates (Tanner, 1962; Douglas and Simpson 1964; Douglas and Blomfield, 1958), since boys who were high scorers on the SAC scale were over-represented in the lower social groups and higher birth orders? Because of smallness of numbers only manual-group boys were considered, and within this group boys who scored 4 on the SAC scale were still significantly lighter in weight when compared with non-delinquents. However, when only fourth born or later manual-class boys were compared, delinquents with non-delinquents, the significance disappeared. The apparent differences in height were also found to be a function of class and birth order.

In addition to heights and weights, shape may be of importance, as much of the earlier work has discussed, but in this study, where shape was expressed as weight for height and was examined in relation to both delinquency and evidence of emotional disruption, in neither case was a significant association found.

DELINQUENCY AND SIGNS OF DISTURBANCE

Five measures of disturbance were available. They were mothers' reports during the primary school years of nervousness, habit behaviour and aggression, mothers' reports to school nurses of habits and symptoms at ages 6 and 11 years, mothers' reports of the child's bed wetting up to age 11 years, and information on the use of the Child Guidance Service.

During these first eleven years of life mothers from time to time made comments to interviewers and on questionnaires about behavioural problems of their children. These largely unsolicited comments have been drawn together, and although they were made by only a part of the population (51.8 per cent) they have been included since a spontaneous comment on this subject is likely to reflect a matter of some importance. They should be seen, like teachers' reports, as indicators of how the mother felt about this child, and thus as one kind of indicator of their relationship.

Future delinquents were more likely than others to be seen as aggressive; this was associated with offences rated 1, 2 or 3 on the SAC scale, but not with offences against other people. Associations between these reports and the two measures of delinquency remained statistically significant only among manual-class families, where more mothers worried about aggression, whilst non-manual mothers most commonly reported that they were concerned about nervousness in their sons. There were no differences in types of behaviour worries when related to whether the family had been broken or not.

School nurses also asked mothers specific questions about worries, particularly concerning health but also about habit behaviour and education; there were no differences between delinquents and non-delinquents in respect of any of these. Nor were there significant differences in the way that mothers handled habit behaviour in delinquents and others, whether they reported using punishment, rewards or particular treatments, or whether they simply ignored habits. Similarly, delinquents were not differentiated from non-delinquents by mothers' reports to school nurses of habits and symptoms at ages 6 and 11 years.

Complete information on bed-wetting is available for 72.5 per cent of this population, and so numbers in some groups are very small. But by the time they were aged 4 years, 73 per cent of the population on whom we have information was dry at night. There was no significant association between this measure and delinquency, although there was a tendency for those who were still enuretic after age 11 years more often to score 4 on the SAC scale.

Child Guidance Clinics were at this time (1950-7) a fairly scarce resource and their use is at any time likely to be both under-reported and a poor measure of need. During this time, sixty-five (3.0 per cent) mothers reported taking the Survey member child to a Child Guidance Clinic; 3.5 per cent of all non-delinquent boys and 2.4 per cent of delinquent boys had been taken to a Child Guidance Clinic.

There has been a suggestion that delinquent boys who score particularly well on intelligence tests are more likely than others to be psychiatrically disturbed (Gath, Tennent and Pidduck, 1970). All of these signs of disturbance were checked, comparing delinquents with non-delinquents amongst both the population whose aggregate test scores at ages 8 and 11 years were in the top and those in the bottom quartiles, and no significant relationships were found. This difference in findings may be because Gath *et al.* used a sample of boys drawn from a remand home population, or the result of differences in measures of disturbance and the younger age of this population when these measures were taken.

CONCLUSIONS

This chapter has shown that apparent differences in physical characteristics between delinquents and others were actually accounted for by social-group and birth order differences between these two groups. There were some indications of differences between delinquents and others in reports of disturbed behaviour during these early years (pre-school, infant school and primary school), but these were very small.

CHAPTER 8

Secondary School

INTRODUCTION

Adolescence generally, and experience of secondary school in particular, has attracted much research attention. Psychologists have seen this as a time of personality development much affected by the onset of sexual maturity. But Wall's (1968) socio-cultural view of adolescence illustrates the relatively recent trend towards an approach that integrates the biological, psychological and sociological views. He stresses the effect of changes in the contemporary social order, and particularly of family geographical mobility, at the same time as the development in personality:

> Many boys and girls arrive at puberty with a thirst for danger and exploration unassuaged in its primitive early forms, with no basic felt understanding of community, without experience of a range of nuanced relationships. It does not seem fanciful (though it remains to be proven) to suggest that some adolescent escapades which result in crime are child's play conducted with adult means, that the exaggerated need to identify with the group is a reaction to a depersonalized and incomplete experience of a human community, and that the attempt to wean oneself from emotional dependence on parents takes the form of outright hostility and rejection of adults because it has not been moderated by other relationships earlier. [p.7]

Much of the more sociologically oriented work has been on the place of the school and the experience of school in the development of an adult role; whilst some have concentrated on the importance of the home and the family of origin in this process (e.g. Douglas *et al.* 1968; Glass, 1954), others have stressed the importance of the school and of the interaction with teachers (e.g. Bernstein, 1973; Jackson and Marsden, 1962).

In this study, information is available about a wide range of adolescent experiences. This chapter examines the association of delinquency with the school physical environment, with scoring on tests of achievement, with teachers' assessments of behaviour and with parental interest. The following chapter looks at personality measures of both the boy and his mother, at signs of 'maladjustment', at the effects of puberty and at a measure of psycho-physiological reaction to stress.

TYPES OF SECONDARY SCHOOL

In 1956 when they were aged 11 years, Survey members moved from junior to secondary school, most of them undergoing some kind of selection for secondary school entry. By the time they were aged 15 years the type of secondary school attended significantly differentiated delinquents from non-delinquents within social groups, with the exception of boys from the upper non-manual social group, where numbers were too small. In each of the other social groups a significantly greater percentage of delinquents was to be found in the less academic secondary modern, bilateral and technical schools when compared with the percentages of delinquents in the more academic grammar, independent and direct grant schools. Within school types the effect of boys' social group of family of origin was modified by the type of secondary school attended, so that at each point on the SAC scale boys from non-manual homes were significantly more often delinquent if they attended secondary modern, bilateral or technical schools than if they went to grammar, independent or direct grant schools, and the same was true for boys from manual homes. Although it is reasonable to conclude that school type does modify the effects of social group of family, there is no way that this can be demonstrated in this study. Thus, the question of the extent to which this modification is the result of something in the school environment or the effect of greater police attention to offences committed by boys from lower types of secondary schools remains unanswered.

Head teachers described the location of their schools, and these were grouped simply into urban and rural; there were no differences in delinquency rates between them. While there were also no differences in rates of delinquency either among those who changed location when changing school, or among those who did not, there was some indication that recidivist delinquents were proportionately fewer among boys who were at rural schools throughout their school careers.

There was no relationship between delinquency and amenities of the secondary school, or between the differences or otherwise in amenities between junior and secondary schools. Nor was there a relationship between the size of secondary school attended and delinquency. Although half of the sample experienced a change in the size of school between junior and secondary, a quarter of the sample going to larger secondary than junior schools, the experience of change in size was also not related to delinquency.

However, the social structure of the secondary school was significantly related to delinquency, with more delinquents and recidivists coming from lowest social-class schools, but this was statistically significant only among non-manual boys.

It was clear that children who were at non-manual schools, both at junior and secondary levels, and those who changed from predominantly manual to predominantly non-manual schools were less likely to be delinquent than all others. Although the act of transition, if it involved a social-class change, appeared to increase the likelihood for non-manual boys of committing a low SAC scoring offence, for manual boys it seemed to reduce the likelihood of committing a higher SAC scoring offence. But these differences were not statistically significant.

The delinquency or otherwise of boys who were selected for grammar school was examined according to whether the junior school of origin was generally reckoned to have high, medium or low success in selection for secondary school places; there were no differences in rates of delinquency according to success of the junior school of origin. When the delinquency of boys at other kinds of secondary schools was checked against success rate at junior school there was a trend towards greater delinquency among boys from low success rate junior schools, and towards least delinquency among boys from higher success rate junior schools, but these differences were not statistically significant.

How far the choice of secondary school matched up with the actual type of school attended is unfortunately known for only 59.2 per cent of non-delinquents and 50.6 per cent of delinquents because many parents could or would not express a wish about secondary school education; so the meaning of these results is difficult to assess.

However, it was found in this depleted group that boys whose parents wanted them to go to grammar school and who did not succeed were significantly more likely to be delinquent than boys who were successful in getting grammar school places. On the other hand, boys who specifically chose to go to non-grammar schools were significantly more likely to be delinquent than those who went to schools that were not their choice.

There were no differences in delinquency as between single sex and co-educational secondary schools. Almost half (45.3 per cent) of boys changed either from or to a mixed sex school, but whether or not there was a change of any kind had no discernable effect on delinquency.

Test Scores

It has already been shown that test scores at ages 8 and 11 years were not helpful discriminators of delinquency, and that although delinquents did less well than expected on the 11-year test the fact of under-achievement was also not very discriminative.

At age 15 years the situation was essentially the same. Three tests were taken (details are to be found in the Appendix), of non-verbal intelligence, of reading and of mathematics and arithmetic, and these were all combined into an aggregate score as before. Once allowance was made for social group and birth order, any significant association between delinquency and test scores was lost. As expected in view of the earlier National Survey work, the arithmetic/maths test showed most relationship with delinquency (Ross and Simpson, 1971a, 1971b) but, although lower than expected achievement on this test was significantly related to delinquency, it was not sufficient to give significance to differences in the aggregate score. Low achievement by boys who committed offences against the person (SAC scale score 4 offences) could perhaps be explained by the fact that significantly more of them than any other group of offenders had not achieved puberty at this age, and it has already been shown that in the National Survey 'boys and girls who are early in reaching sexual maturity are superior to the late maturing children in tests of mental ability and school performance' (Douglas and Ross, 1964).

Parental interest in secondary school education

Just as parental interest in primary school education was scored with the use of a combination of teachers' assessments and parents' reports, so parental interest in secondary education was assessed in the same way at two points during the secondary school years, when Survey members were aged 13 years and again at age 15 years, and this measure was, as before, combined into one rating of parental interest.

This measure was very significantly related to delinquency and also, as Table 8.1 shows, to the SAC scale. The same level of statistical

TABLE 8.1   *Teachers' ratings of parental interest in boys' secondary school education, and the social acceptability of crime scale*

Parental interest rating in quartiles	Social acceptability of crime scale					Total (=100%)
	0 no crime	1	2	3	4	
Lowest	65.8	3.0	15.8	10.2	5.3	266
Second	87.1	2.4	5.0	4.2	1.4	505
Third	88.2	2.7	4.8	2.9	1.3	373
Highest	92.0	1.3	5.1	1.1	0.5	376

$\chi^2 = 109.10$ with 12 d.f. $p < .001$

significance was also achieved in each social group. In view of what is already known, both from this investigation and from many others, this result might have been expected. Low parental interest in the child's education and school life is in most cases likely to be a real reflection of low parental interest in other aspects of the child's existence, and it was therefore not surprising to find that the level of parental interest was closely related to family structure and circumstances, as well as to measures of achievement. Boys who at age 15 years were in large families were, in both social groups, significantly more likely to have lower parental interest scores than boys who were only children, and the proportion of lowest interest scoring parents rose progressively with each increase in family size. Low parental interest was also significantly more characteristic of broken families, whenever the break had occurred, when compared with families that were not broken, especially if the type of break was divorce or separation; this again was statistically significant in both social groups. Boys of parents rated as low in interest also had significantly low scores on the aggregate of the 15-year test scores.

The relationship between parental interest and delinquency remained significant in both types of secondary school, but in the secondary modern, bilateral or technical secondary school the association remained only for manual social-group boys.

It may be that teachers' assessments of parental interest are affected by their knowledge of the child and of the family. For example, perhaps the low rating of parental interest contained some element of self-fulfilling prophecy and maybe teachers 'expected' lower interest from these parents. In some way perhaps, lower test scores were also 'expected' from boys whose parents received low interest scores. In order to see how far this was so, the effect of teachers' knowledge of delinquency was removed by examining only the relationship between parental interest and delinquency committed *after* the interest rating was made. This involved the exclusion of 60.3 per cent of delinquents, and when this was done the relationship was still statistically significant.

As in chapter 6 it is not possible to say how many correctly discriminated delinquents and non-delinquents this assessment added to the totals given by the use of family data because of the problem of missing information from these later years.

TEACHERS' VIEWS OF BEHAVIOUR

When boys were aged 13 and 15 years teachers rated their behaviour using a postal questionnaire comprising twenty-one three-point assessments (see Appendix). For the purpose of analysis the assessments were grouped under six headings: (1) ability, (2) tidyness, (3) influence of outside factors, (4) relationships with the teacher, (5) relationships with other pupils, and (6) the summary assessment. Teachers also indicated how well they felt they knew the Survey child: at 13 years only 5.3 per cent of boys were said to be 'not very well known' to the assessing teacher; at 15 years the proportion was 4.9 per cent. There was no class difference in acquaintanceship, nor were delinquents any less well known than others, although the percentage who were least well known rose with increasing family size. Only the assessments made at age 13 years were used, since not only were these slightly more in number than those made at the later age, but also by using them a greater number of boys could be considered who were not yet delinquent at the time of this assessment. Two assessments were made only at age 15 years and these have also been used. These assessments should be regarded in the same way as teachers' assessments made in the primary school years (discussed in chapter 6), which were seen not as objective measures but as indicators of the teacher's relationship with this child.

Delinquents came off badly on each assessment, even when the delinquents considered were those who first committed an offence after these assessments were made. They were significantly less likely to be regarded as able to benefit from whole time study after leaving school and more often assessed as untidy and unpunctual. In relationships with the teacher, delinquents were said to be more often resentful of criticism, disobedient, restless in class and given to daydreaming; they were also seen as more difficult to discipline in comparison with others and more prepared to lie to evade trouble. In their relationships with other children at school, delinquents were significantly more often assessed as liable to get unduly rough at play time, as more dare-devil and, but less often, as more fearful than the average child. In addition, they were more often said to experience factors outside school that adversely affected school work. In their overall character assessments, teachers more often felt those who were later to become delinquent to be aggressive. Although aggressive boys more often scored 3 or 4 on the SAC scale, in fact those assessed as aggressive accounted for only 16.4 per cent of all who later achieved these scores and 9.1 per cent of those who later scored 1 or 2.

As well as delinquents, of course, others received poor teachers' assessments, especially boys from large manual social-group families. Those rated as untidy and unpunctual, unduly resentful of criticism, frequently disobedient, prone to restlessness and daydreaming, difficult to discipline and prepared to lie to avoid trouble had also significantly more often experienced a family break, been rated as poor or lazy workers at primary school, scored in the bottom quartile of the aggregate test scores at age 11 years and had parents rated in the lowest quartile of interest in their education. This was also true of boys assessed as rough or dare-devil. Since such background factors and attributes were characteristic of delinquents and of boys who were low rated, the question therefore is were these assessments simply picking out the large manual social-group families and thus happening to get the delinquents too, or were they so related to delinquency that they could discriminate the delinquents in any social group or family size? Multiple regression analysis was used to assess the contribution of these assessments to the discrimination of delinquents from non-delinquents once the effects of the intervening factors had been accounted for. In this event only some assessments remained significant: often being late for school and lessons, lying to avoid punishment, disobedience in class, roughness, being a dare-devil and suffering the effects of adverse factors on school work. However, despite their significance, the total contribution of these assessments to the explained variance was slight. Altogether these variables explain 36.76 per cent of the variance, but of this 26.12 per cent was contributed by the intervening variables of social group, family size, family break, parental interest in education, attainment and ability test scores and adjudged attitude to work at primary school. A discriminant analysis showed that these variables added no 'new' delinquent cases to those already correctly discriminated by the intervening factors.

DISCUSSION

In common with other researchers this investigation has found very little or no relationship between delinquency and the school physical environment, or the type of school attended or the Survey member's score on attainment tests or any test designed to measure ability, even when the boy's official delinquent career first began after leaving school. The most notable relationship was with an indicator of parental interest in the child's secondary school education. Of less significance was the relationship between later delinquency and teachers' assessments of a child's behaviour in class and with his fellow pupils.

These findings will come as no surprise, but the question remains as to how they should be interpreted. West and Farrington (1973) have referred to 'pre-delinquent behaviour', which of course, and along with all other behaviour observed before delinquency was recorded, is logically true. However, this does not seem to be a particularly helpful classification, and it is likely to be more fruitful to consider ratings and assessments in their relationship with other knowledge collected earlier in the lives of Survey members since, as West and Farrington themselves say, 'if background factors existing before pre-delinquent behaviour are predictive, this is an important clue to possible causes' (p. 131).

Teachers undoubtedly really did find manual-group boys from large families more troublesome in class, more disobedient and less punctual and tidy. But it is hardly likely that such features are an inherent part of being a member of a large manual-group family. It is more likely to be a product of two processes. First, the association of these ratings with low attainment scores and with poor ratings of attitude to work at primary school indicate that boys who were seen as troublesome at age 13 years very often already had a poor reputation. Second, reputations are perpetuated by the person concerned 'living up to his image', and it is evident from the work of Hargreaves (1967) that this is not an uncommon process in secondary schools.

He concluded of the behaviour of a boy observed in his investigation as having the least favourable report possible that

> ... much of it was true. Whenever possible, he would shout wildly and distract or provoke other boys. Most of his time at school was spent in a search for distractions. He would laugh openly if a teacher told him that his school work would help him to get a good job. . . . This behaviour represents an adaptation to a situation. In part it is a necessary adjustment to a situation in which he is a member of a stream whose members are penalized in favour of upper and especially A streams. He has learned to be seen as a relative failure. His relationships with teachers deteriorated steadily over four years until he was totally rejected by many. He made virtually no progress at his work. In short, the allocation of teachers, the tendency for teachers to favour higher stream boys, and the kind of relationships teachers made with the boys contribute in a fundamental way to the values of the boys. [pp. 100-1]

In discussing how teachers of low streams cope with discipline problems among lowly motivated pupils, Hargreaves wrote that:

> The first mode of adaptation is that of *withdrawal*. Because this type of teacher (i.e. low stream teacher) is less competent in matters of discipline yet is assigned to forms with the greatest discipline problems, he avoids the problem by ignoring its existence. He does this by sitting in his desk at the front, marking boys' work or some similar activity whilst the rest of the class continue to enjoy the relative chaos which reigns. . . . The second mode of adaptation for the less competent teachers with low streams is that of *domination*. This type of teacher imposes a

completely rigid discipline, infringements of which incur severe penalties. Because silence reigns in the form the children appear to be working hard. In reality, they make little effort; they become increasingly bored by the lesson, their interest in the subject declines, and they seek to undermine the authority of the teacher by disturbing the lesson without being apprehended. [pp. 103-4]

Reputations are also perpetuated by word of mouth among teachers in staffroom discussions. Boys regarded as intelligent or hard working or stupid or lazy by one teacher are likely to have this view of them passed on in staffroom chat, particularly if they are seen, as delinquents characteristically are seen, at one extreme or other of a particular range, such as intelligence.

Rather than interpreting with West and Farrington (1973) their observation that different teachers gave similar ratings of pupils, as giving support to the 'objectivity' of the rating, it should surely be seen as evidence of the social stereotype of the boy as it exists in that school. As Hargreaves (1967) found:

> . . . inferences which the teacher draws in such a highly selective way from the pupils behaviour, and the 'categorisation process' to which it leads, act as a definition of the situation in which teachers and pupils find themselves. This definition provides the plan for all future interaction between the two parties. Because the inferences are selected from limited aspects of the child's behaviour and are interpreted in terms of the teacher's role expectations there is a constant danger of misinterpretation. The teacher may draw conclusions which are unjustified when we consider the totality of the child's behaviour. [p. 105]

A similar process may well have been at work in the case of the assessments of parental interest. By the secondary school years, and especially when as at this time (1959) the selective school system operated, parents will be well aware of their son's image at school, both in terms of classroom behaviour and achievement. Parents of delinquents may very well feel that displays of interest in education by visiting the school and discussing progress will be a humiliating and probably fruitless exercise.

It looks as though these two important factors from the secondary school years owe a lot to teachers' interpretations of boys' lives at school and to their views of boys' and parents' lives at home before this time; the wider implications of this are discussed in the final chapter.

CHAPTER 9

Personality, Behaviour Assessments and Physical Development during the Teenage Years

INTRODUCTION

This chapter examines the relationship of delinquency with three sorts of information. First, relationships with personality measures are examined, both the personality of the boy at age 13 and 15 years and the personality of the mother. Next is considered the importance of certain behaviour that psychologists often classify under the general heading of 'adjustment', for example habit behaviour and mothers' and teachers' reports of 'nervousness' and 'aggression'. Finally two physical measures are examined. The state of physical maturity or puberty at age 15 years is included because of its relationship with behaviour, and pulse rates at age 11 years are also considered since a number of other studies have shown them to be related not only to offending and to deviant behaviour but also to emotional circumstances.

TWO MEASURES OF PERSONALITY

The relationship of personality measures with delinquent behaviour continues to arouse considerable controversy. Eysenck has been the chief proponent in this country, and his view of criminal behaviour was expressed in *Crime and Personality* (1964):

Criminality is obviously a continuous trait of the same kind as intelligence, or height, or weight. .... It would be meaningless to talk about the criminality or otherwise of a Robinson Crusoe, brought up and always confined by himself on a desert island. It is only in relation to society that the notion of criminality and or predisposition to crime has any meaning. [pp.62-3]

Eysenck begins from an assumption of innate predisposition to crime, which he sees as managed by a control mechanism regulated by conscience, which in turn 'is the combination and culmination of a long process of conditioning'. Sociologists would point out that 'socialisation' is a continuous process, by no means stopping at some point in childhood. Eysenck continues:

It is suggested that socialised behaviour rests essentially on a basis of conditioning which is applied during a person's childhood by his parents, teachers, and peers, and that his conduct in later years is determined very much by the quality of the conditioning received at that time, and also by the degree of conditionability which he himself shows; that is to say, the degree to which he is capable of being conditioned by stimuli which are presented to him. [pp.99-100]

The degree of conditionability is said to vary, extroverts being least receptive and therefore those with the least conscience; in addition, a high degree of neuroticism strengthens the individual trend to either extroversion or introversion. Eysenck predicts, therefore, that criminals are extroverted and emotionally unstable, and moreover that they have a tendency to psychoticism (Eysenck and Eysenck, 1970), a factor comprised of such characteristics as solitariness, cruelty, aggression and attention-seeking.

Two of the many levels of discussion in progress about this hypothesis should be considered here. They are both concerned with testing the hypothesis and not with questioning its derivation, and they therefore begin from the point of using the designations 'neuroticism' and 'extroversion'. The first level on which discussion takes places is that of questioning how a hypothesis that has been almost entirely built on comparative studies of offenders in custody and control and be said to be adequately tested and understood until the effects of selection of populations for prosecution and custodial disposal is taken into account. Cochrane (1974) has been the most recent person to make this point, which has, so far, not been adequately answered. The data available in this study are not able to tackle all aspects of this question because of the absence of self-report data on crime. They are helpful, however, in examining three problems associated with this hypothesis: is neuroticism/extroversion related to offending in this sample? is neuroticism/extroversion related particularly to any type of crime? is any prediction by neuroticism/extroversion affected by other intervening variables?

Two kinds of measures of neuroticism/extroversion were used in this study. The first was Pintner's rating (Pintner, 1938), a list of forty-five statements with yes or no answers, which was self-completed by 1729 (78.7 per cent of all boys) boys at age 13 years. The second measure was the short (twelve item) version of the Maudsley Personality Inventory (Eysenck, 1958), which was self-completed at age 16 years by 1680 boys (76.5 per cent). The MPI is a well-known and documented inventory, but it is perhaps necessary to make some comments about Pintner's rating. Mulligan (1964) has said that in this study:

> The Pintner was chosen in preference to other inventories, from a limited and poor field . . . It does not contain tough, prying items of a kind likely to arouse protest from parents or teachers. There was a risk that in choosing a relatively soft-treading questionnaire efficiency and validity might thereby be lost. [p.37]

Delinquents were more often rated as neurotic on Pintner's rating whatever their classification on the introversion/extroversion axes, and although there was no statistically significant relationship between delinquency and introversion/extroversion, there was between delinquency and neuroticism when using the SAC scale. Although in this population significantly more neurotics on Pintner's measure were in the manual social group and significantly more neurotics were from the fourth birth order or higher, the neuroticism score remained significantly related to delinquency for all birth orders and in both social groups. Multiple regression analysis showed that once birth order and social group were taken into account Pintner's rating of neuroticism still contributed significantly to the discrimination of delinquents from non-delinquents, both when neuroticism was considered alone and when neurotic extroverts were isolated as a special group.

The MPI was also significantly related to delinquency, but this was true only for the neuroticism scale. Unlike Pintner's rating, the MPI score was related neither to social group nor to birth order. Neurotic extroversion seemed most powerfully associated with SAC scores 3 and 4, but the influence appeared almost as powerful among those who scored in the middle range of both neuroticism and extroversion. Clearly, it is necessary to question the relationship of the Pintner to the MPI measure, and to ask how far they could be said to be 'measuring' the same things. Neuroticism scores correlated slightly better (r = .285) than those of extroversion (r = .224) on the whole population, but they only correlated significantly in the non-delinquent population, and at no level of the SAC scale; on the other hand extroversion scores correlated significantly in the non-delinquent population and in those scoring 1 or 2 on the SAC scale, but they were not significantly correlated in the population scoring 3 or 4.

In order to compare the relative usefulness of these two measures of personality they were used in a stepwise multiple regression analysis together with social group and birth order to test their power to discriminate non-delinquents from delinquents. After the effects of social group and birth order had been taken into account only Pintner's measure of neuroticism continued to make a significant contribution, followed by Pintner's measure of extroversion. Neither of the MPI measures contributed significantly to the discrimination of delinquents from non-delinquents.

From these results it was evident that Pintner's ratings and the MPI were not measuring the same things, and two explanations can be offered. First, Pintner scores are related to social group, whereas MPI scores are not. This may be because of the length of the Pintner (forty-five statements compared with twelve on the MPI) and because it was completed at a younger age (at age 13 years as compared with the MPI at age 16 years), when possibly reading and concentration were less good and boys may, therefore, have been more inclined to mark the schedules with less care. Second, the questions concerned with neuroticism, in particular, seem to be qualitatively different. Some of the Pintner statements tap a dimension that the MPI does not, namely that of fright or fear, with such statements as 'I worry about getting ill' and 'I am afraid of thunder'. Unfortunately, it was not possible to analyse the Pintner data omitting these sorts of statements, nor was it possible to do other than regret that only the short version of the MPI was used.

A measure of the mother's personality

When Survey members were aged 15 years their mothers gave answers at interviews with school nurses or health visitors to a short version of the Maudsley Personality Inventory (Eysenck, 1958), which comprised a scale of six questions designed to give a rough and ready measure of neuroticism or emotionality. In this cohort Douglas *et al.* (1968) found that

> the mothers who, on a shortened version of the Maudsley Personality Inventory show a high proportion of statements associated with neurotic behaviour, are more likely to see themselves as being in poor health than those who rejected these statements. Thus only nine per cent of women in good health had high neurotic scores on the inventory compared with twenty six per cent of those in poor health. [pp.92-3]

and that

> . . . those whose mothers have high neuroticism scores on the Maudsley Personality Inventory are more likely to leave [school] early. A high level of parental interest, high employment ambitions for the child and a good record of visits to the school on the part of the father are all associated with longer school life. [p.181]

In view of Rutter's (1966) findings of the importance of parental physical illness on the mental health of their children, and particularly of sons, neuroticism scores of Survey members' mothers were examined in relation to delinquency and in relation to factors already shown to be associated with delinquency. Although those boys who were found to be neurotic by the Pintner Inventory (Pintner, 1938) were significantly more likely than others to have mothers whose answers to these six questions showed them to be very neurotic, there was nevertheless no relationship between this measure of mothers' personality and delinquency. Nor was there a relationship between this measure and family breaks or types of break.

BEHAVIOUR ASSESSMENT

Mothers' and teachers' spontaneous reports

As in the primary school years mothers' and teachers' spontaneous and unsolicited comments on the Survey child's behaviour were recorded during the secondary school years, and although they were small in number (181 or 8.2 per cent of mothers made comments, and so did teachers about 140 or 6.4 per cent of boys) the fact that the mother or a teacher thought it appropriate to mention them was regarded as a sign of their importance; it could, of course, also simply be a result of rapport between the interviewer and the mother.

Mother's reports can be grouped into those of nervousness and habits, and those of aggressive behaviour (leaving six children as unclassifiable). When they were restricted to those who were first delinquent only after age 16 years there was no relationship between these reports and delinquency. However, teachers' assessments were significantly related, and boys who were yet to become delinquent were more commonly rated as having nervous, habit or aggressive behaviour. Unfortunately, numbers were too small for this group to be split into the two sorts of behaviour, and, of the 124 delinquents, mothers and teachers rated 5.6 per cent as aggressive as compared with 3.3 per cent of non-delinquents, and 16.9 per cent as having habit and nervous behaviour as compared with 14.5 per cent of non-delinquents. Mothers more often than teachers reported boys as aggressive, but less often reported them to have habit or nervous behaviour. Both mothers and teachers significantly more often rated boys whose homes were broken when they were aged 0-4 years as having either habit or nervous or aggressive behaviour, and teachers rated boys from homes broken at any age as more often behaving in these ways.

Symptoms and signs of maladjustment

Douglas *et al.* (1968) found that the presence of the symptoms examined here was related to neuroticism, and that 'the more adverse items reported the lower is the performance in school' (p.116). It was therefore worth examining their relationship with delinquency. In the National Survey, six measures have been taken to be symptoms or signs of maladjustment:

(1) A list of symptoms (nose picking, stammering, nail biting, tics and general fidgetiness, unexplained vomiting and abdominal pain, bed wetting, thumb sucking and any other habits) which was asked of the mothers by doctors or nurses and separately of

teachers when the Survey member was aged 5 years, 11 years
and again at 15 years.

(2) Mothers' reports of the child's nightmares or disturbed sleep at
ages 6, 10 and 11 years.

(3) A question put to mothers by the school nurse or health visitor
when the Survey member was aged 15 years about whether he
had been to 'an outpatient department at a hospital clinic for
nervous or disturbed behaviour' since he was 11 years old. This
information has been supplemented by reports of psychiatric
treatment received during these years.

(4) Replies by teachers to questionnaires sent through Local
Education Authorities both when Survey members were aged
13 and 15 years about whether they truanted.

(5) Replies by teachers to postal questionnaires when Survey
members were aged 13 and 15 years about whether they cheated
in class work.

(6) Mothers' and teachers' spontaneous comments about adjustment.

Neither the information about nightmares (2) nor that concerning
hospital treatment for psychiatric or disturbed behaviour (3) were
related to delinquency, but it should be noted that in both cases the
prevalence of these was very low. Only 1.9 per cent of boys had been
to a hospital outpatient department for this sort of treatment, 3.4 per
cent had received some kind of psychiatric or child guidance help
and 10.9 per cent had had nightmares or disturbed sleep, 9.9 per cent
occasionally and 1.0 per cent once a week or more often. Of the three
sets of symptoms asked of the mother (1) only those asked at age 15
years were related to delinquency, although the set asked at age 11
years shows a similar trend. At age 15 years delinquent boys were
significantly more likely to be reported as having two or more of the
symptoms, but this significance did not hold if boys first delinquent
after age 16 years only were considered. The incidence of these
symptoms was not related to family breaks, but it was significantly
related to neuroticism, as measured on the Pintner scale, such that
those with two or more symptoms were more neurotic than others.
Even when the effects of Pintner's measure of neuroticism and social
group and family size were accounted for, reported symptoms at age
15 years still contributed significantly to the discrimination of
delinquents from non-delinquents.

Truancy (4) was a rare event, particularly at age 13 years when only four (0.2 per cent) boys were said to have been 'frequent' truants and a further fifty-eight (2.6 per cent) were 'occasional' truants; this may be because we have used the teacher's definition of truancy. By age 15 years 'frequent' truancy was to be found among eighteen (0.8 per cent) boys, and it was 'occasional' among seventy-one (3.2 per cent). At both ages truancy was, not surprisingly, both statistically significantly more frequent amongst delinquents and twice as common among non-manual social-group boys as among manual boys, and it remained significantly more common among those who, at these ages, had not yet been officially designated delinquent. Of the eighty-eight boys (4.4 per cent of the population of non-delinquents and delinquents who first offended at or after age 16 years) who had truanted, only nine (10.2 per cent) were said to have done so at ages 13 *and* 15 years, and only two of these were later delinquent.

Cheating in class work or cribbing (5) was at both ages more often reported of manual social-group boys than others, and it was also found significantly more often among those who were still to become delinquent than those who were not. It was more often reported than truancy (26.7 per cent of boys), although here too only a small number of boys (thirty at age 15 years and twenty-three at 13 years) were said to be 'frequent' cribbers. Cribbing was more often associated with the later non-indictable rather than later indictable offending, and this was the case at either age. Similarly, cribbing was more common among boys scoring 1 or 2 on the SAC scale (36.1 per cent of boys with this score were cribbers at age 15 years) than among boys scoring 3 or 4 (29.5 per cent were cribbers) or boys who were not delinquents (19.1 per cent). Boys who were said at both ages to have cribbed were a little more likely to be delinquent than boys who were only said on one occasion to have cribbed.

PHYSICAL DEVELOPMENT

Puberty

Since heights and weights have already been discussed, only two physical factors are considered here, namely ages at onset of physical maturity and a measure of psycho-physiological reaction at age 11 years.

One of the most important events for boys aged 11 to 15 years is puberty. Those whose facial hair comes latest and whose voices remain squeaky and higher than those of their class mates may well feel embarrassed and socially ill at ease at this time. They may be particularly vulnerable because as Hargreaves (1967) observes this is a time when 'young people tend to fall back on the peer group, for it is with their age-mates that they most interact and from whom independent status may be derived'. Other visible signs of late onset of sexual maturation are absence of or relatively sparse growth of axillary and pubic hair and shortness of stature, although the latter is more obvious as a statistic than in the observation of a particular child in everyday life. We know, too, that invisible but equally important hormonal changes associated with the onset of sexual maturity can be emotionally disturbing. So it is not unreasonable to look at the relationship of puberty with delinquent behaviour.

In this study, doctors conducting a medical examination especially for Survey members at age 15 years assessed 1753 boys (79.8 per cent of boys in this sub-sample) for signs of physical maturity (see the Appendix for details of assessments). Boys rated at this age as having infantile physical maturity were significantly more likely than other boys to be delinquent, this was true only in those from manual social-group families, regardless of whether the secondary school attended was of mixed population or of boys only. Similarly it was only in the manual social group that the stage of physical maturity achieved at 15 years was related to the SAC scale, as Table 9.1 shows, with proportionately more physically infantile or early puberty boys scoring highest, and proportionally more physically mature

TABLE 9.1 *State of physical maturity at age 15 years, and the social acceptability of crime scale (manual social-group boys only).*

State of physical maturity	Social acceptability of crime scale				
	0 no crime	1	2	3	4
Infantile	9.1	16.0	16.2	18.9	26.1
Early puberty	34.7	12.0	27.5	41.5	34.8
Advanced puberty	31.4	48.0	27.5	24.5	26.1
Fully mature	24.8	24.0	28.8	15.1	13.0
TOTAL ($=100\%$)	795	25	80	53	23

$\chi^2 = 21.14$ with 6 d.f. p $<$ .01 (adding SAC scores 1 and 2, and 3 and 4)

boys scoring lower. There were no significant differences in mean age at first offence as between the four puberty stages, but manual social-group boys who were fully physically mature at age 15 years appeared to have a slightly younger than average age at first offence. Of all the sixteen boys who scored 4 on the SAC scale and who at age 15 years were either in a stage of infantile physical maturity or only showing signs of early puberty, nine committed sexual offences, and these account for more than half of the seventeen boys who committed sexual offences.

However, despite its significant relationship with delinquency, the state of physical maturation at age 15 years did not contribute significantly to the discrimination of delinquents from non-delinquents once social group, birth order and height had been taken into account in a multiple regression analysis.

Inevitably great care needs to be taken in the interpretation of these findings, particularly since some of the factors associated with age at onset of physical maturity are also related to delinquency. Earlier work from the National Survey found, along with many others, that 'children from small families reach puberty on the average at a younger age than children from large' (Douglas *et al.*, 1968, p.138), and that earlier puberty was characteristic of taller boys and of boys who were only children. It is clear that these are all factors more often found among non-manual group boys, and it has already been demonstrated that these factors are also associated with a reduced chance of later delinquency. Therefore, in assessing the real importance of stage of physical maturation at age 15 years, the influence of these factors must also be taken into account. A stepwise multiple regression analysis showed that once the effects of these other variables have been taken into account the state of physical maturity at age 15 years did not contribute significantly to the discrimination of delinquents from non-delinquents.

But despite the outcome of this last regression analysis it is important not to overlook the association with later delinquency of those few boys (105 or 6 per cent of those assessed) who were still in an infantile state of sexual maturity at 15 years of age. This is evidently a relationship that requires further and more detailed investigation to ascertain how this might be accounted for by social and psychological factors, or whether glandular development *per se* is of importance. These late maturing boys could well be outcasts in the social world of school.

Pulse rates

On the face of it pulse rates would seem an odd thing to investigate in the study of delinquency. However, there has been a considerable amount of investigation of associations between functioning of the autonomic nervous system and anti-social behaviour (see Wadsworth, 1976, for a selected bibliography). These studies of autonomic functioning all seem in some measure to agree with Tong and Murphy (1960) that 'faulty fear responsiveness to stress is at the basis of continual psychopathic instability'. Other studies of psychopaths that have been concerned with antecedent family history have noted that early emotional deprivation is a very common feature of later psychopathic behaviour (McCord and McCord, 1964). Early emotional deprivation is, of course, also known to be a common feature of those who later become delinquents. This led Davies and Maliphant (1974) to suggest that 'stress in early childhood may contribute to such atypical autonomic activity'. Certainly from the published work it would be reasonable to speculate that children who in early life lived in surroundings of stress and emotional disturbance are more likely to develop some mechanism for handling the effect of such stress, and this may be reflected in later autonomic reaction to stressful situations.

At a school medical examination that took place when Survey members were 11 years old, medical officers were asked to note pulse rates per minute before the physical examination. These examinations were arranged specially for the children, who were singled out from their class mates at the time of the appointment. Before the pulse rate was taken children waited while their mothers answered a maximum of thirty-three questions about the child's health. This period of waiting in anticipation of the medical examination is regarded as a source of stress, possibly strengthened in many cases by the fact that the child had no prior knowledge of what was to take place, being the only one involved, and deprived too of the comfort of knowing that others were undergoing the same examination. Certainly these data were not collected in ideal and standardised conditions, either in terms of the way in which the doctors took pulse rates or with regard to the usefulness of the medical examination as a stressful event, although at the age of 11 years it may well have been more stressful than in older persons. Standardisation would have been impossible since the examination took place in 3060 schools at the same time.

Pulse rates of offenders were found to be significantly lower than those of non-offenders, and so also were those of boys from homes broken while they were aged 0-4 years. Among those who had not experienced a break at home, the pulse rate of those later committing offences against others were significantly lower than those of all other offenders and non-offenders. Pulse rates of 84 beats per minute or below were found in ten (66.7 per cent) of the fifteen cases of those committing sexual offences, and in seventeen (80.9 per cent) of the twenty-one cases of those committing violent offences that were not of a sexual nature. Of 1544 non-delinquent boys, 54.3 per cent (838 boys) had pulse rates within this range. Although discriminant analysis using the pulse rate data and information on social group, birth order and Pintner's measure of neuroticism (Pintner's non-neurotic introverts had significantly higher pulse rates than others) yielded a statistically significant discrimination of the two populations, it only classified 57.5 per cent of all boys correctly, either as delinquents or non-delinquents; thus 52.5 per cent were classified incorrectly. However, of the thirty boys in the sub-group who had committed sexual or violent offences nine (30 per cent) were misclassified as non-delinquents and twenty-one (70 per cent) were correctly classified as delinquents; of the twelve boys who committed sexual offences, six were correctly classified and six incorrectly, but only three of those who committed violent offences were misclassified and fifteen were correctly classified. Therefore, although the discriminative power of these variables was low in distinguishing delinquents from non-delinquents, their strength evidently lay in their ability to distinguish particular kinds of delinquents, namely those who had committed offences involving violence against persons.

CONCLUSIONS

Of the two personality measures used in this study only the Pintner was found to be related to delinquency, and the measure of neuroticism was the most important feature of this association. A rating of the mother's personality was not associated with delinquency, and neither were six indicators of 'maladjustment', although in the latter case numbers were very small. Of all the physical data available, the pulse rates in a stressful situation were most important in discriminating delinquents from others, particularly those who committed a violent offence. Boys, whether delinquent or not, who had a low pulse rate reaction to stress at age 11 years were significantly more likely to have experienced a broken home in early life, and the importance and interpretation of this finding are discussed in the concluding chapter. Although age at achieving physical and sexual maturity was not significantly associated with delinquency, there was an unexpected greater frequency of offenders who were still in a state of infantile physical maturity at age 15 years, and it is suggested that this finding would be worth follow-up in other study populations.

CHAPTER 10

Delinquency in Girls

INTRODUCTION

The most striking fact about official delinquency in girls is how little there is in comparison with delinquency in boys. When this study population was aged 20 years (in 1966), observed guilt findings per 100,000 of the total English and Welsh population of that age were 2700 for men but only 266 for women. This difference is itself quite sufficient to make it worth comparing delinquency in males and females in a sample where the same data have been collected for both sexes.

Offending rates for women up to age 21 years in this study were comparable to those for women of the same age in the total English and Welsh population, and the overall rate among girls in the study population was 2.0 per cent before statistical weighting to compensate for sample bias (as compared to 15.3 per cent of boys) and 2.46 per cent thereafter (17.9 per cent of boys). As in most studies, the mean age at first offence for girls was older than that for boys, being 15.6 years as compared with 14.7 years in boys. As Tables 10.1 and 10.2 show, there were proportionately fewer girl recidivists and proportionately fewer girl offenders who scored 3 and 4 on the SAC

TABLE 10.1 *The distribution of boy and girl offenders, observed and weighted (in brackets)*

	Non-indictable offences	One indictable offence	More than one indictable offence	Total (=100%)
Boys	30.7	47.0	22.3	336
	(27.3)	(46.1)	(26.6)	
Girls	17.5	67.5	15.0	40
	(13.6)	(73.7)	(12.7)	

TABLE 10.2   *The distribution of boy and girl offenders on the social acceptability of crime scale, observed and weighted (in brackets)*

| | Social acceptability of crime scale | | | | Total |
	1	2	3	4	(=100%)
Boys	15.1	46.4	26.7	11.8	330
	(13.6)	(46.5)	(27.3)	(12.6)	
Girls	10.0	77.5	10.0	2.5	40
	(8.5)	(82.2)	(8.5)	(0.8)	

scale, i.e., who had committed the *least* socially acceptable offences. This is also the case on a nationwide scale (McClintock and Avison, 1968). The one girl who had committed a violent offence was convicted of assault occasioning actual bodily harm and was bound over to keep the peace. As the SAC scores indicate, most offences by girls were against property and did not involve breaking in (see Appendix for the list of offences). As well as these girls who offended against the criminal law, six others (104 per 100,000 after weighting) were brought before the courts as being beyond parental control, and a further two (250 per 100,000 after weighting) were taken into care because of their mothers' long-term illness. Only three of the forty delinquent girls received custodial treatment, one going to prison and two to approved schools.

As with the boys it is unfortunate that illegitimate children were not included in the sampling of this cohort.

EXPLAINING SEX DIFFERENCES IN CRIME

Like the greater part of the research literature on crime in males, the work on women and crime has usually been based on studies of populations already arrested and in institutions. The disadvantages this confers by ignoring the effect of the differential application of police and judicial procedures have already been discussed, and they apply here as much as they do in studies of males.

Discussions of crime committed by women who have also been constricted by an inevitable and particularly close concentration on things that are unique to women, especially physical factors. Unfortunately, environmental factors have been restricted mainly to information about home conditions. The argument that the 'cause' of female criminality could not be environmental, because of the lack of similarity in the crime rates of men and women, has been based on a narrow definition of environmental factors, and is only now just beginning to be challenged. I shall argue that this challenge is of the greatest importance.

Physical factors

Physical differences have, naturally enough, been regularly searched for explanation from the earliest work of writers such as Lombroso (1895) and Thomas (1907). They were concerned with the supposed passivity of women, evidence for which they found in sexual activity, comparing the conventional role in sexual intercourse, the activities of sperms and ovaries and the maternal instinct. Evidence for passivity was also seen in the relatively small numbers of women statesmen and great artists. When roused from this passivity for some reason, it was argued, sexual offences such as prostitution occurred and even greater violence than in men (Pollack, 1961). Other specific physiological factors cited as acting by disorienting or distracting the sufferer so that she loses her normal social control are, of course, menstruation, the menopause and pregnancy (Dalton, 1961; Gibbens and Prince, 1962; Pollack, 1961). More recently Cowie *et al.* (1968) have argued that greater physical size is a predisposing factor towards delinquency, noting that delinquent girls in their institutionalised sample tended to be 'over-sized, lumpish, uncouth, and graceless' (p. 64), and they suggest that this difference in size may be indicative of chromosomal abnormalities. They also implicate genetic factors in suggesting that 'the type of crime into which [she] may drift, and the extent to which [her] life is governed by [her] criminal tendency, would seem to be largely a reflection of [her] personality, with genetical factors lending much that is most characteristic' (p. 174).

Psychological factors

Cowie *et al.* (1968) also argue that girls are less often delinquent than boys because they are better able to tolerate stress, but as Mannheim (1965) observed psychiatric hospitals have an over-representation of women, even though he saw this as predisposing them 'to some greater extent to be deprived of the opportunity to commit crimes' (p. 707). Rates for admission to English psychiatric hospitals per

100,000 of the total population in 1974 were 307 for men and 425 for women. Cowie *et al.* noted the predominantly unstable and emotionally cold homes of their series of girl delinquents, and 'the large number of girls of very good intelligence' (p. 77), in contrast with their frequent 'educational deprivation'.

Social factors

Delinquent girls are often said to be not particularly competent at social relationships. Wattenberg and Saunders (1954) reported this as a common feature, and so did Cowie *et al.* (1968) when the social relationships were those taking place within the family. They found the

> ... clearest impression that what has gone wrong is the family and home as a unity. In one considerable group home life is unhappy and distorted by intolerable conflict, the parents estranged, or governed by rigidity and restrictions, or isolating the girl in an affectionless world. In another equally important group one sees disintegration, or the children going their own way, no contact with the parents, who can give no supervision or support, chronic insecurities caused by many moves, many schools, no roots, the home comfortless, overcrowded, squalid, or simply chaotic. Children from such homes are brought before the magistrate again and again, with equal punctuality being sent back to them again, for further neglect, or further harm. [pp. 164-5]

In a similar way Schofield (1968) in his notable work on sexual behaviour found that those girls who were sexually experienced during their teenage years (i.e. those who behaved in a way that did not receive general approval) had an antipathy to family loyalty and a dislike of home restrictions. When compared with boys '... a girl is more influenced by her family loyalty' (p. 208). However, in view of the findings of Cowie *et al.* that boys when compared with delinquent girls come from homes with 'worse discipline' and 'more conflict' and 'more disturbed intrafamilial relationships', perhaps reports of difficulties in social relationships are not surprising. Nye (1958) also found broken homes to be significantly more common among girl delinquents than other girls, and in reviewing the literature Cowie *et al.* concluded that 'girl delinquents deviate from social and psychological norms much more than boy delinquents' (p. 166). Some writers, among them Nye (1958) and Cowie and her colleagues (1968), have also discussed the importance of the relative lack of opportunity for offending by girls because of stricter parental control, and although this has changed of recent times it will have been an important factor when these authors were writing, and when the girls in this study were teenagers, that is from 1958 to 1965.

Social factors beyond the home and family seem to have been little considered until recently, with the exception of Mannheim's (1965) discussion of law making:

> Men seem to have made penal laws mainly to prevent and punish actions which they thought endangered their personal interests, whereas certain specifically female forms of misconduct were often regarded as not serious enough or too pleasant or indispensable to them to warrant penal measures. The legislators, being males, may unwittingly have moulded the whole system of criminal law in such a way as to turn a blind eye to some of those anti-social actions most frequently committed by women. . . [p.691]

But social factors are now being invoked in attempts to explain the apparent narrowing of the difference between male and female crime rates in Western urbanised countries. For example, Nettler (1974) reports that 'in the United States during the ten years from 1960 through 1969, the robbery rate for males under 18 years of age increased 170% while the rate for females increased 319%' (p. 103). Such observations, although no doubt accurate, may be misleading if used to argue for a spectacular increase in female crime, since as Radzinowicz and King (1977) note, 'translated into absolute figures, the 89% rise in the crimes of Brazilian women represents little more than a thousand extra offences, whereas the 43% rise amongst men represents over 14,000' (p. 17). Nevertheless, it does seem to be a very widely experienced phenomenon.

> In the United States arrests of women over the period from 1960 to 1972 rose almost three times as fast as those of men. The trend extended not only to larceny but to such hitherto unfeminine pursuits as robbery, burglary and embezzlement. In Germany the female share in recorded crime rose, in only 7 years, from 15.4% to 17.1%. In Canada it doubled in 9 years, from 7% to 14%. In Japan it rose in 10 years from 9.8% to 13.6%. Norway and New Zealand report similar trends. [Radzinowicz and King, pp. 15-16]

Assembling social information to account for such changes seems an obvious course to take, but defending the choice of information used is a difficult task. A feature common to those countries where female crime rates are rising is the increasing social and economic independence of women. Although it could be that these social circumstances have changed the social behaviour of women in ways that make them more likely to commit crimes, the importance of changing societal views of women's roles must not be overlooked. Just as these views give an opportunity for greater independence, so they will also be affecting police and judicial processes. Smart (1976) reports a comment by Smith (1975) that 'the recent increase in officially recorded violence amongst girls suggests that a change in definition, rather than in behaviour *per se* has already taken place' (p. 72); and Smart comments that 'the police, social workers and other agents of social control are more ready to define deviant behaviour by women and girls as violent or "masculine" because of apparent changes in the social and economic position of women in society' (p. 73). It is of course impossible to know how far either of these changes accounts for the rise in crime amongst women, but they both emphasise the need for studies of social behaviour to consider the effects of the views of others, and the actors' own perception of others' views.

FINDINGS IN THIS STUDY

Because of the small number of delinquent girls, they were compared with their non-delinquent fellows by matching with controls for birth order and social group, unless otherwise stated. Each matching operation was done twice, and any statistically significant trend is reported only if it occurred in *both* sets of controls. The definition of delinquency used is the same as that used for boys, which was described in chapter 2. In comparing the present findings with those of others it must be remembered that delinquent behaviour in this study does not include such things as truancy or sexual promiscuity, unless these acts have involved an infringement of the criminal law.

Home circumstances and family life

The forty delinquent girls in this study came from predominantly manual social-group families; thirty-four had fathers who at the time of their birth were in skilled or semi-skilled work and the remaining six fathers were clerical workers. When compared with controls matched for social group, delinquent girls were less likely, but not significantly so, to have been only children. To compare the physical home circumstances and family life of delinquent girls with others they were first matched for social group and birth order, and after this no differences were to be found in home physical environment of delinquents compared with others. However, as with the boys, family circumstances were of importance: by age 15 years, twelve (31.6 per cent of the thirty-eight families for whom information was available) delinquent girls came from families that had experienced some kind of disruption because of the permanent absence of a parent during this time, as compared with four (10.5 per cent) of the controls. Eight of the twelve delinquents from broken families (as compared with two controls) had experienced a family break as a result of death of a parent or their divorce or separation by the time this child was 5 years old. Comparison of boy delinquents with girl delinquents shows that although experience of a broken home has an important effect in both sexes, it is not in fact the same. Of all delinquent girls, 20 per cent came from families broken by divorce, separation or parental death before they were aged 5 years as compared with 10.7 per cent of boys; and 26.3 per cent of delinquent girls experienced these sorts of family breaks between birth and age 15 years as compared with 17.9 per cent of delinquent boys. Since numbers of children from the control group broken families were so small, the effects of remarriage could not be estimated.

Mothers of delinquent girls were married at a significantly younger age (mean 20.2 years, S.D. 2.51) when compared with others (mean 23.4 years, S.D. 5.05) even when matched for social class, but they were not significantly younger at the birth of the Survey child, although fathers were. Mothers of girl delinquents were significantly more likely to go out to work during the Survey child's first six years of life when compared with other mothers, but there was no difference in the number of months during which they were employed. There were no significant differences in age at which mothers first worked, but mothers of delinquent girls more often changed their jobs (nineteen did so as compared with ten controls) and they worked significantly longer hours per week while the children were in their first six years of life.

Physical differences

After matching for social group, birth order and completed family size, delinquent girls were compared with others to look for differences in age of achievement of certain developmental milestones (age at walking and talking), their heights and weights at six different ages, age of achievement of puberty (see Appendix) and a ranking for shape (expressed as the cube root of weight divided by height) at age 11 years and 15 years. Of these only the age of achievement of puberty showed an interesting but not statistically significant association: delinquent girls reached menarche later than others — only nine (27.3 per cent) had reached menarche by 14 years and 10 months or later, as compared with seventeen (42.5 per cent) of non-delinquents.

School

Delinquent girls were again matched with others for social group, birth order and completed family size, and differences in test scores sought in various tests of verbal, non-verbal and mathematical ability and achievement taken at ages 8, 11 and 15 years (see Appendix for details). No significant differences were found. The school environment, its amenities and its type were also not associated with delinquency in girls, and neither was the age at which parents expected their daughter to leave school, nor the job they hoped she would take. In these things girl delinquents were similar to boys, but they were different in the matter of parental interest in education and in teachers' assessments of classroom behaviour. Although these were all powerful discriminators of boy delinquents, both at primary and at secondary schools, for girls at primary school only the rate of parental interest showed a similar trend, but did not reach statistical significance. The ratings at secondary school were so often not available for delinquent girls that interpretation of such scant data was not attempted. Delinquent girls were also significantly more absent from secondary school when compared with others.

Measures of personality and signs of disturbance

Like the boys, girls completed two personality assessments, the Pintner (Pintner, 1938) and the short MPI (Eysenck, 1958), and their mothers also took the short MPI when their Survey member child was aged 16 years. The short MPI taken by the girls showed a significant excess of delinquents among the extroverts but no difference among the introverts. On the other hand, the Pintner inventory showed an excess of neurotics but no difference among the extroverts. Assessments of behaviour disturbance in girls were the same as those used for boys (see chapters 6 and 8), and included the incidence of nightmares and bedwetting, as well as mothers' reports of habits at ages 6 and 11 years, but none of these were associated with delinquency.

Discussion

Delinquent girls were differentiated from others by some of the same factors that differentiated delinquent boys from their non-delinquent age peers. Like boys, delinquent girls were apparently particularly affected by the experience of life in a family broken by parental death, divorce or separation before they were aged 5 years; among delinquent boys 10.7 per cent had experienced life in this kind of disrupted family by this age and so had 20.0 per cent of delinquent girls. For boys this was associated with crimes committed against other people, but for girls there was no association with any particular type of crime, perhaps because the types were all so similar — only four of the forty girls had committed breaking and entering offences (SAC score 3) and one had committed an offence against another person (SAC score 4). But it is important to note that although broken homes have a strong and significant statistical association with delinquency, nevertheless neither in boys nor in girls do broken homes 'account for' more than a small proportion of all delinquency. Of all boys from such homes disrupted by the time they were aged 5 years, 28.6 per cent were delinquent by the time they were 21 years old; the figure for girls who had this experience was 7.9 per cent. The fact that this kind of disruption is important in delinquency both in boys and girls makes it worth further investigation. Now we need to ask very specific questions about why this association should exist, how an experience at such an early age could have an effect on behaviour so much later on in life, and why it is largely associated with one kind of delinquency in boys, but with another kind in girls. These questions are discussed in the next chapter.

The whole question of the differences in crime rates as between males and females seems not to be answered in any way by the life history data collected in this study, since were it to be so there would have to be factors that clearly differentiated female delinquents from other girls and that did not differentiate male delinquents from other males, and *vice versa*. But certainly the factors that do differentiate delinquents from others in either sex do not have equal effects. And this, of course, is a clue to at least two other areas that would be worth exploring: maybe girls cope with stress in ways that are dissimilar from those used by boys, or perhaps society expects different behaviour from boys and girls from these backgrounds. These possibilities are also discussed in the concluding chapter.

CHAPTER 11

Conclusions

Probably the commonest and most widely recognised problem in studies of delinquency is that any group of officially designated delinquents cannot be a representative sample of all those who break the law. This, it is argued, makes a mockery of studies of delinquents, since decisions about who gets officially labelled delinquent and who does not are obviously taken by policemen. If this were so then looking for differences in the lives and characteristics of delinquents as compared with non-delinquents would be fruitless; really we should investigate police methods.

But studies of police methods show that the reality is not quite so straightforward, and draw our attention to the role of the public both as witnesses or bystanders and as victims; for example, Black and Reiss (1970) found that a little more than three-quarters of events involving police and juveniles were initiated by public complaint. I have already argued (in chapter 1) that police views of the 'seriousness' of crime, and their scaling of interest in crime, reflect commonly held public views, and this is supported by studies of victims as well as complainants. Many kinds of offence are seen as not worth reporting, not only by the victim but also by bystanders and the police. For some, and in certain circumstances, this may be an unwillingness to get involved in the tedious business of making statements, waiting to give evidence, possibly having time off work to attend court proceedings and, perhaps, even a fear of reprisal. But even these things are determined by views of the seriousness of the crime concerned.

Thus, actions that technically constitute a breach of the law, do not actually become offences until they are so defined by the actions of others. In the self-report studies it is the lack of information on the social context of reported events that makes it impossible in many cases to tell which of them might *ever* have been regarded as crime. This may not be necessary if we are estimating the national loss

through shoplifting, or fare dodging, but it is important in considering the size of the so called 'dark statistic', or crime not reported
to the police. Its importance lies in the fact that the dark statistic will
vary from crime to crime because of police and public views about
seriousness. Offences that are not considered to be particularly
serious will be under-reported, and therefore can be expected to
have a considerably larger 'dark statistic' than those that are generally
seen as unacceptable.

Because of this, the present study used a social acceptability of
crime scale in which a score of 1 indicated that all the guilt findings
reported for this individual between ages 8 and 21 years comprised
only victimless and non-acquisitive offences, which were judged to
be the most socially acceptable, whereas a score of 4 showed that this
person had injured or seriously sexually offended another person.
It was proposed that for the same reason that some offences are least
socially acceptable they are correspondingly 'difficult to commit', in
that their commission involves going against widely held views that
regard such offences as most abhorrent and unacceptable. It was
hypothesised that those delinquents with the most acceptable SAC
scale scores would be least representative of offenders of this kind,
and that those with the most unacceptable scores would be most
representative. Unfortunately this could only be tested on boys
because of the small number of girl delinquents.

With this scale, and with the National Survey's advantages of a
wide range of social, psychological and medical data collected
without the encumbrance of recollection from a large and representative population, the life histories of delinquents and non-delinquents have been compared. An aetiological approach was used to
test established hypotheses and the value of prediction. That is, it
was used to see:
(1) if the conventional criminological findings were replicated on
    contemporaneously collected data, and if so whether the
    associations found were the same for all offenders on each of the
    four points of the SAC scale; and
(2) incidentally, how far the conventional criminological idea of
    'prediction' actually works on a population sample, rather than
    on a population with matched controls.

FINDINGS

The most striking findings concerned family life, where disruption of parent-child relationship in early life, through parental death, divorce or separation, was associated with later delinquency, and chiefly with the most unacceptable kinds of offences. Unfortunately we have no information about families in which emotional disruption may have occurred but not led to divorce or separation. Large family size was also associated with these kinds of SAC scale scores, and conversely being an only child seemed to have a significantly protective effect against delinquency. These associations were not accounted for by the family's social group, or home physical environment or health visitors' (community nurses) assessments of the mother's care and management of this child. Although whether or not the mother went out to work during the child's first six years of life seemed not to be associated with delinquency in boys, girls whose mothers worked particularly long hours at this time were more inclined to be delinquent.

School life, on the other hand, was a less fruitful source of associations with delinquency. The measures of ability and achievement taken at intervals in both primary and secondary education did not distinguish delinquents from others and neither did details of the school physical environment. However, boys who experienced a favourable ratio of pupils to teachers at primary school (i.e. where there were relatively fewer pupils for each teacher) had a reduced chance of delinquency. The type of secondary school attended was important, in that the less academic schools had the greatest proportion of delinquents, whatever their social group. But the most striking associations in the information about schools and delinquency were to be found in the teachers' assessments of behaviour. Boys assessed at primary school as average, poor or lazy workers were significantly more likely later to be delinquent, and so were those assessed as having parents with little interest in their school life. This was also true of secondary school: boys who were seen as disruptive and disobedient were more often either already delinquent or became so later, but this finding was of little discriminative power compared with secondary teachers' assessments of parental interest. The difficulties encountered in attempts to interpret this sort of data were discussed in chapter 8.

Information on physical characteristics was, with two exceptions, not associated with delinquency in either boys or girls. Pulse rates of boys assumed to be under stress were significantly lower if they had experienced family life in a broken home before the age of 5 years. Age at achieving puberty or sexual maturation (see chapter 9 for the indicators used) was not statistically significantly associated with delinquency, but boys and girls who had still not achieved puberty at 15 years were more inclined to become delinquent.

Personality inventories yielded only relatively slight associations with delinquency, and neuroticism was the most important component in boys and girls. Mothers' and others' reports of habit behaviour, nightmares and bed wetting were of little significance.

The hypothesis that those male delinquents with the most socially acceptable scores would be least well discriminated from non-delinquents, and those with the least acceptable scores best discriminated was demonstrated to be correct. Although some factors did distinguish the 61.6 per cent of all offenders who scored 1 or 2 on the SAC scale, these boys were virtually indistinguishable from non-offenders in the multivariate analyses. Conversely those with scores indicating low acceptability were best discriminated. Table 5.3 gave the rates of prediction achieved by certain family life data for each score on the SAC scale, and shows how discrimination improved as crime became less socially acceptable. But, as Table 11.1 shows,

TABLE 11.1   *Discrimination of delinquents and non-delinquents (actual numbers)**

	Predicted as delinquent	Predicted as not delinquent
Actually delinquent	136	50
Not in fact delinquent	711	915

* Using data on birth order, family size and growth, parental divorce, separation or death by this child's fifth birthday, prolonged or frequent hospital admission by this age, social group

however good individual types of discrimination may have been, overall prediction was poor, with 36.8 per cent of delinquents not correctly identified and, worse, 43.7 per cent (711 individuals) of non-delinquents wrongly identified as delinquent. Since the statistical method used in this analysis maximised chances of good discrimination this was a disappointing result. When the analysis was set to discriminate delinquents giving them a chance equivalent to their proportion of the total population (that is rather than giving delinquents and non-delinquents equal chances of discrimination) specificity and sensitivity were even less satisfactory. To look for clustering of delinquents the cutting point was moved to include only the 25 per cent of the population discriminated as most likely to be delinquent; 47.8 per cent of delinquents came into this best discriminated or predicted sector, but so did 22.4 per cent of non-delinquents (Wadsworth, 1978). But the findings are not surprising in view of the relatively small proportion of delinquents discriminated by any one of the factors considered. Even information on the disruption of family life while the child was less than 5 years old, which was significantly associated with later delinquency, showed that over two-thirds (69.3 per cent) of boys who had this experience did not become delinquent.

DISCUSSION

The importance of information on family disruption in the early life of the child is the most striking finding, especially since the data available overcome most of Wootton's (1959) points about methodological difficulties in such investigations. They are also in agreement with the findings from West and Farrington's (1977) longitudinal study that what seem to be adverse experiences in early life do not apparently have 'their full effect until age seventeen to twenty' (p. 157). But why should an event that occurs ten or more years before a particular kind of behaviour be in any way associated with it? As Kagan (1976) observes, such a concept of continuity between events in early life and behaviour in later life, or what he calls 'psychological epigenesis', is practically traditional in psychology, but relatively little work has been undertaken to demonstrate its validity.

In this study there is some evidence to support two hypotheses about this association. First, suppose that it exists because children living in disrupted families have to learn to handle stress much more often than others, and that this leads them to react differently to it in later life. The findings on boys' pulse rates support this hypothesis. Boys who had experienced an early family break had a lower pulse rate reaction to stress when compared with others. Once early emotional disruption had occurred, pulse rates of both non-delinquents and delinquents were similarly low. Pulse rates in girls, however, are not noticeably different, according to family experience or type of crime committed.

The findings on pulse rates, coming at age 11 years, a little over half-way in time between the experience of family disruption and the particular kind of delinquent behaviour with which it is most strongly associated, may be a clue that, at least in boys, coping with stress is affected by such family disruption experienced before age 5 years in that their reaction to stress still seems to be affected some six years later.

But if this effect is so powerful and so long lasting we should expect to see its manifestation in ways other than delinquency. Perhaps some express this effect in behaviour that comes in various ways to be called delinquency, while others do so in other ways. This may help to explain why girls seem less often to have a delinquent 'outcome' when compared with boys. Perhaps girls more often express this effect in ways other than delinquency. It therefore seemed worthwhile to examine available indicators of how stress was handled in later life by comparing experiences of a number of illnesses often said to be associated with stress or emotional disturbance and certain personal circumstances that may also be seen in this way, as between those who had a disrupted family life in childhood and those who did not. The illnesses were psoriasis, migraine, asthma, epilepsy, stomach and duodenal ulcers, colitis (as an adult) and psychiatric disorder, which had received hospital inpatient treatment by age 26 years. The family circumstances were a divorce or separation by age 26 years and in girls an illegitimate pregnancy by this age. It has already been shown (Wadsworth, 1978) that those boys who were discriminated by the data on early life disruption as delinquent but who were in fact not so, were more likely to have been admitted to psychiatric hospitals by age 26 years (23.9 per thousand as compared with 14.2 per thousand of those predicted as not delinquent), and they were also more likely to have experienced stomach or duodenal ulcers or colitis by this age (25.3 per thousand as compared with 7.7. per thousand in predicted non-delinquents). Table 11.2 shows for both men and women those circumstances and illnesses in which there was a notable association with family disruption in early life, and it shows too the apparent importance of family disruption at this time in the child's life, not

TABLE 11.2 *Experience of certain illnesses (if admitted to hospital), delinquency and divorce or separation by experience of parental death, divorce or separation in family of origin (only those living in England or Wales at age 8 years are included)*

Experience	Age at which family disruption occurred						No disruption	
	0-4 years		5-15 years		16-26 years			
MALES *Total no. experiencing family disruption*	126		149		238		1683	
	%	No.	%	No.	%	No.	%	No.
Delinquency by 21 years	28.6	36	16.1	24	16.0	38	14.1	238
Stomach ulcers or d colitis by 26 years	1.6	2	0.7	1	0.4	1	0.4	7
Psychiatric illness by 26 years	6.3	8	2.7	4	0.8	2	1.7	29
Divorce or separation by 26 years	1.6	2	4.0	6	2.1	5	2.4	40
% of total who experienced the events above*	36.5	46	22.8	34	18.5	44	17.9	301
FEMALES: *Total no. experiencing family disruption*	116		152		273		1494	
	%	No.	%	No.	%	No.	%	No.
Delinquency by 21 years	7.9	8	2.6	4	1.5	4	1.6	24
Stomach ulcers or colitis by 26 years	—	0	—	0	—	0	0.1	2
Psychiatric illness by 26 years	3.4	4	3.3	5	4.0	11	1.5	22
Divorce or separation by 26 years	11.2	13	5.9	9	4.8	13	3.1	46
Illegitimate child(ren) by 26 years	6.0	7	4.6	7	5.9	16	3.9	59
% of total who experienced the events above*	23.3	27	16.4	25	16.1	44	9.6	143

* Percentages and totals don't add up since some individuals experienced more than one of these illnesses and family circumstances

only for delinquency but also for other circumstances. Admission to psychiatric hospital seems to be associated with early family disruption, particularly in men, but this may to an extent be a self-fulfilling prophecy, since because of the importance of emotional disturbance in early life in many theories of psychiatric disorder, psychiatrists may be more inclined to admit individuals with such experience to hospitals. Marital breakdown by age 26 years seems not associated for men, but in women this and illegitimate pregnancy are more often associated with family disruption in early life than at any other time. Whilst taking these findings as partial confirmation of this hypothesis it should nevertheless be noted that such family disruption in early life is by no means an inevitable or especially powerful predictor of these things in later life, at any rate up to age 26. At its best in men it 'accounts for' 36.5 per cent of these circumstances and illnesses, and in women only 23.3 per cent. Nevertheless it is disruption in the earliest years that seems most strongly associated with these later illnesses and types of behaviour. Those men who had lived through a family disruption by divorce, separation or parental death by their fifth birthday were twice as likely to experience more than one of these things when compared with all other groups of men in Table 11.2 (1.6 per cent of those experiencing early breaks had more than one of these things): five delinquents (1.5 per cent of all male delinquents) had also been admitted to psychiatric hospitals by age 26 years, and thirteen (3.9 per cent) had been divorced or separated. Women who had lived in a disrupted family before their fifth birthday were four times as likely to experience more than one of these things when compared with all other groups of women (4.3 per cent of those who experienced early family breaks had more than one of these things): by age 26 years, seven girl delinquents (17.5 per cent) had had premaritally conceived illegitimate children and four (10.0 per cent) had been divorced or separated. The fact that the proportions of men and women apparently affected by the experience of an early family break are quite similar, and yet within each of these chosen indicators of outcome (i.e. the illnesses and family and personal experiences used in Table 11.2) the proportions vary considerably, may be a reflection of differences in the social acceptability of different kinds of behaviour in men and women. This might also be the explanation for the association of early family disruption in males with violent and sexual offences, while in females it is associated with more acceptable crime, since for women law-breaking is a much less socially acceptable form of behaviour.

As a second hypothesis it could be argued that such associations might in any event partially be accounted for by generally held social views of the effects of disrupted family life. Teachers rated boys and girls from broken homes as significantly more often poorly behaved at school, with a low interest in learning, poor classroom behaviour and having parents who showed little interest in their education and school life. Just as the basis of the social acceptability of crime scale was general public 'knowledge' of the cause of crime as lack of parental discipline (see Banks *et al.*, 1975), so the importance of general 'knowledge' about child-rearing as affected by broken family life should also be taken into account. Perhaps at the basis of the teachers' assessments was their 'knowledge' of the effects of a broken home, particularly of divorce or separation. In 1954, when the children in this study were at primary school and first being assessed for attitude to school work, Bowlby's studies of the effects of maternal deprivation were already published in paperback, and of course the academic work had already been published in journals. *Forty Four Juvenile Thieves* was published in 1944, and Burt's work, which had been first published in 1925, had already concluded that

> of environmental conditions, those obtaining outside the home are far less important than those obtaining in it; and within it, material conditions, such as poverty, are far less important than moral conditions such as ill discipline, vice, and most of all, the child's relations with his parents. [p. 607]

Contemporary books for social workers discussed 'the serious harm done to children whether the home be broken by divorce or by other cause' (Mayer, 1946, p. 18), and concluded, for example, that 'the basic cause, seen by everyone with experience of these children, is lack of unity and happiness in the family. Nothing, more than this, can be so utterly destructive to the moral fibre of the child who falls its victim' (Watson, 1950, p. 31). And in 1951 a World Health Organisation expert committee advocated that the use of day nurseries was likely to cause 'permanent damage' to emotional health (WHO 1951). Still in 1965, incidentally, delinquency was to be found as officially recognised with a coding number in the World Health Organisation's International Standard Classification of Diseases, Injuries and Causes of Death.

The Clarkes (1976) note in particular the danger inherent in an easy acceptance of this 'knowledge', especially for social workers, since 'the wholesale acceptance that poor experience in the first few years inevitably leads to doom has [also] tended to set in motion administrative decisions which confirm the implication' (p. 23). But how much more damaging must it have been for teachers to have such 'knowledge', which could be applied to all children not just those who come into contact with social workers? Teachers will have 'known' of the damage done by a broken home because of this general folk 'knowledge', and also because the many books already published at this time on the effects of maternal deprivation invariably form part of the recommended reading for teachers in training, as well as for social workers.

There is evidence from this study that teachers and health visitors did indeed regard boys from broken homes rather differently. In chapters 5 and 6 it was shown that not only did teachers and health visitors give significantly more adverse ratings of school behaviour and maternal care to those who had already experienced a family break caused by divorce or separation, but they did not distinguish children whose homes were in fact in future (by their fifteenth birthday) to be broken in this way. We do not know whether health visitors and teachers were actually aware in each case that the family had had this experience; and it is, of course, impossible to quantify how much application of general 'knowledge' about effects of such an experience contributed to a boy becoming delinquent, but it is reasonable to expect that these views will at least have acted as reinforcement, in the Clarkes' sense. This is not because of overt labelling. I have simply used these views in this study because they are available as an illustration of what I speculate were generally held social views about and expectations of effects of broken homes on children, particularly on young children. I suggest that the effects of such views could be seen in changes in the individual's self-concept and in perception of self as rather different when compared with others. It may be, therefore, that in this way children from homes broken during their pre-school years actually suffer more stress in later life than other children.

It might be objected that, valid though these findings may be in themselves, there is reason to think that family life is now rather different from when Survey members were in their early years, with possibly less emphasis now on the mother-child relationship. It is also true that divorce is now considerably easier to achieve, separation is likely to be more common since it is so much more socially acceptable, and parental deaths are proportionately fewer, especially in the early life of the child. However, although family life certainly has changed, there is no reason to suppose that either the emotional or the physical attachment needs of children have changed. Nor is there reason to believe that the need for parental interest in and encouragement of children has diminished, or that there has been a reduction in the common view that children of necessity suffer ill-effects when they experience a broken home.

Divorce and separation are still likely to be as much of an upheaval in family relationships as they ever were, and the time preceding the separation is as likely now as ever to be fraught with quarrelling and emotional upset. Illsley and Thompson (1961) point out that 'the circumstances leading to a broken home and the continuity and quality of care following the break seem. . . to be more important than parental loss itself'. It is regrettable that we do not have more sensitive information about parental relationships, whether or not families experienced a *de facto* separation.

Thus, there is support from this study for both of these hypotheses about why certain kinds of delinquents, more commonly than chance would lead us to expect, come from a family that was broken by parental divorce, separation or death before the fifth birthday of the child. There is support for the view that it is because such emotional experience somehow influences the child's manner of coping with stressful situations and, as is shown in Table 11.2, these children, more than any others, experienced certain illnesses and behaviour often associated with emotional disturbance. But there is also some support for the hypothesis that contemporary views about and expectations of the likely effects of early life in a broken family will have had a self-fulfilling effect, because others' views of such children will affect their life circumstances and chances and also their self-concepts. There is, of course, no reason to suppose that these findings are incompatible, because there will be as many explanations as there are degrees of family emotional disruption. It may be that others' views and expectations and the child's developing self-concept are more often the agents that increase the chance of experiencing the illnesses and kinds of behaviour as shown in Table 11.2 than is the actual experience of the emotional disruption. It could very well be that the personal experience of particular social views may bring about such a change; and there is plenty of evidence of links between social and emotional circumstances and physiological and metabolic adaptation, as for example in the failure to thrive syndrome, and in many studies of psychophysiological interactions (see, for example, Liederman and Shapiro, 1964; Raab, 1971). It may even be that some are born to parents who are themselves somehow predisposed to emotional instability, and who in turn genetically predispose their children to react to stress in a particular way, but this study has no evidence either to support or refute this proposition. These are all subjects for further study.

THE USEFULNESS OF THESE FINDINGS

Can life history information predict delinquency?

What have these findings to offer that is of immediately practical value? A glance at the nature of the information collected is enough to make it clear that there is neither sufficient detail nor large enough numbers of delinquents in any of the four categories of the social acceptability of crime scale on which to base conclusions that would be safe enough to use in the treatment of individual cases. But such conclusions are rare from a single research project, of course, not only in the social sciences but also, for example, in medicine. Prediction of certain future heart disease from a few items of information on diet, exercise, blood pressure and body measurements would be very insecure, but the relative likelihood of such an outcome could be established from a population study using such information, and relative likelihood of outcomes is a basis for considering preventive action.

In this study it is evident from the numbers of false positive and false negative discriminations shown in Table 11.1 that any kind of direct intervention that used this sort of information to prevent delinquency would be unthinkable; many people would be wrongly predicted to be at risk of delinquency if it was tried.

The findings so far discussed concern the differentiation of non-offenders from those who committed the least socially acceptable offences, that is those who scored 3 or 4 on the social acceptability of crime scale. However, more than half (62 per cent) of the offenders scored 1 or 2 on the scale, and for them significant associations with life history data were few. In fact, the data's success at discriminating them from true non-delinquents was little better than might have been achieved by tossing a coin. This, of course, was not wholly unexpected. It was anticipated (in chapter 2) that since these kinds of offences were generally committed by many people, and that since reporting of them was low, many actual offenders would never officially be classified as offenders, so that obtaining a 'pure' group of non-offenders would be just about impossible. Of course, the failure of the life history data in this study to discriminate these kinds of offenders from non-offenders may be because the information simply did not comprise the appropriate facts. On the other hand, it may be that life history anyway has little to do with this kind of offending and that these kinds of crimes are committed much more from impulse or in response to particular opportunities, especially since committing them is not generally regarded with much disfavour, particularly by age peers. It seems that these offenders could usefully be seen as opportunists, or what Radzinowicz and King (1977) call 'marginal offender(s)':

> Economists talk about marginal producers — those who will come in when the profits are high and the risks are low and who will be the first to drop out if the profits fall or the risks rise. Perhaps we have also marginal offenders, and perhaps it is these who are the main target of general deterrence. [pp. 135-6]

As Mayhew *et al.* (1976) observed, 'there is ample scope for criminologists to consider also the extent to which deviance may be a tempered response to the provocations, attractions and opportunities of the immediate situation', and if over half of those officially regarded as offenders by age 21 years really are marginal, in this sense, then this is an indicator of a need for different approaches to both research and prevention. Research into these kinds of offences should take more account of the immediate social circumstances at the time of the offence itself, rather than concentrating in a traditional way on 'background factors' from early life; these measures or indicators of social circumstances should be less structured than is usual, and should aim to describe not only the offender's social circumstances in some considerable detail (e.g. not inferring life style from social-class ratings), but also the processes of how he or she was arrested, charged and prosecuted. Prevention of such relatively easily committed crimes might usefully concentrate more on such measures as restricting the availability of weapons and having caretakers and community groups in housing estates where vandalism is rife (Newman, 1972). The *process* of acquiring an aura of vulnerability or even propensity to a certain kind of behaviour, which I have suggested happens to children from families broken in a particular way at a certain time in their lives, may also happen on a larger social scale, for example in the acquisition of reputations by housing estates. As Baldwin and Bottoms suggest (1976), much more careful work needs to be undertaken into the commonly observed differences in crime rates between adjacent urban areas.

Could there be any future in further investigation of psychophysiological measures?

Further research is also needed into the meaning and importance of psychophysiological measures. Although the measure of pulse rates used in this study was very crudely taken, the significance of its association with delinquency, and particularly with those who later committed the most socially unacceptable offences, and the significance of its association with early emotional disruption need to be examined in a more closely controlled study. The fact that the associations were not significant for girls also requires further investigation. But if psychophysiological measures could in due course be shown to indicate the *extent* or degree of emotional disturbance, by comparing measures before and after different kinds of emotional upset, they would indeed be valuable.

Are these findings out of date?

It could be argued that these findings are completely out of date. After all, since so much emphasis has been placed on human relationships, and particularly family disruption, it could be objected that such things, and commonly held views of them, have changed. As already noted, divorce is much more readily obtained now and attracts far less social disapproval than in the late 1940s and 50s when these children were young; more girls are now officially described as delinquent; ways of bringing up children have changed very considerably, and so have the courses that train teachers and social workers.

But the particular value of this study is that it accurately reflects the social impress of its time, and it is for this reason that the findings are not out of date. In fact, they might in one respect only just be becoming useful; if they could be compared with those of a similar study carried out on a population born twenty or thirty years later, certain unique research opportunities would result. Such a comparison would give us the opportunity to disentangle the effects of social views and expectations from those of personal attributes and predispositions. It is only by such time-sampling that these basic questions can be tackled. Fortunately an opportunity to do this will present itself if the means are found to continue the follow-up study of babies born in England, Wales, and Scotland in one week in March 1970 (Butler, *et al.*).

What are the indicators for further social and psychological research?

It might generally be concluded from this study that there is little point in treating delinquency as a homogeneous phenomenon, as the use of the social acceptability of crime scale has shown. It seems clear that further research should concentrate on particular kinds of crime, and on some of the things associated with particular kinds of crime, such as emotional disruption in early life. But it also seems worthwhile embarking on a broader kind of social research about crime. By suggesting a need for studies of social views of crime I intend to imply something with a wider social context than the investigations already published on how legal and judicial processes operate. Sociological views of how crime is 'caused' (that is, in a sense generated as well as defined) have been too narrowly focused on social-class and economic issues. Crime is a product of society, in that things that disrupt society and that are particularly contrary to its basic values are defined as crimes. But crime is also defined by social circumstances, both by the immediate social circumstances of the offending behaviour (as discussed in the opening chapter) and by contemporary views of what is right and what is wrong, of what is acceptable behaviour and what is unacceptable.

Thus, studies of the views of acceptability of behaviour are required. The strongest arguments for these that can be put forward from this investigation are to be found not only in the use of the social acceptability of crime scale but also in the sex differences in delinquency rates. Essentially, associations of life history data with later delinquency were the same for both males and females. Delinquency in both sexes was particularly associated with certain family circumstances, especially emotional disruption at an early age, and yet rates of delinquency were very different, being seven times greater for boys. Of recent time the differences in male and female crime rates show signs of narrowing. Evidently differences in social attitudes to behaviour in boys and girls are important and need to be further investigated. Studies of the acceptability of behaviour could continue the work of Banks *et al.* (1975) in delineating public attitudes to crime, so that changes over time could be monitored. They would also need to investigate the 'knowledge' and views held by teachers and social workers about experiences, like broken families, that are commonly held to be damaging to the young child. A longitudinal study of the acquisition of such views or 'knowledge' during the course of training of teachers and social workers would be particularly helpful. It would also be important to have detailed studies of child-rearing, as another reflection of society's views on the acceptability of behaviour. As Miller and Swanson (1958) observed in their pioneering study of upbringing and of changes in patterns of upbringing, 'new methods of child care are likely to spring from new social conditions that. . . have an impact on parents' (p. 5).

If the importance of social views and their changes over time is acknowledged, and if it is accepted that the findings of this study are not outdated, then it would be reasonable to conclude that social acceptability of behaviour and the definitions of crime and delinquency are not static concepts, either in time or in a cultural sense. Views on the necessity of being brought up within a family of two parents and child(ren) are not common to all cultures. In a study comparing ethnic groups within New York city, Simcha-Fagan *et al.* (mimeo), for example, found that 'such variations among groups reflect differences in the role of the father and, moreover in the sanctions associated with his absence in various groups'. Cross-cultural comparisons would certainly be useful. It would be fruitful to investigate childhood emotional disturbance, as defined both by our Western urbanised standards and by the standards of other cultures. This would not only help us to describe differences in views of what causes disturbance, but more importantly enable us to see if the things we suspect of doing emotional damage to children are actually similarly damaging in another cultural setting. At the same time we could see whether events that other cultures see as emotionally damaging to children are also associated with later socially unacceptable behaviour, and with signs of social and personal distress or disturbance manifest in social behaviour and illness experience. Such studies would go a long way towards unravelling the problem of alternative explanations for findings on family disturbance and later behaviour already discussed in this chapter, and expressed as two hypotheses, one largely concerned with cultural transmission and the other with psychological continuity. Of course, various aspects of these proposals have been studied before, especially by anthropologists. But it seems true to say that a study has not yet been carried out to investigate these particular questions.

An international review of 'where we have got to' in delinquency research also seems to be necessary. Such a review would surely show, as the findings of this study show, that investigations of delinquency have too readily and too generally used the concept of psychological epigenesis, apparently in the hope that it would 'explain' all crime. But the role of the social context of crime has been relatively under-investigated. In the last decade, so much has been invested in medical, social and psychological research into this costly problem that such a review would be useful in directing further research, by helping it to capitalise on past experience. It should also encourage research to move away from the traditional academic subject boundaries and to take account of notions in more than one discipline, including the large amount of sociological and philosophical thinking about crime and its causes.

Appendix

Year	Survey member's age	Type of contact and main purpose
1946	8 weeks	Health visitor administered questionnaire to mothers about the confinement and subsequent child care.
1948	2 years	Health visitor administered questionnaire to mothers about the child's health, development and use of services and parental health.
1950	4 years	Health visitor administered questionnaire to mothers about the child's health, development and use of services and parental health.
1952	6 years	Medical examination by school doctor. School nurse administered questionnaire to mothers about the child's health, development and use of services and parental health.
1953	7 years	Medical examination by school doctor. Questionnaire sent to teachers about school type, amenities, child's progress and parental interest.
1954	8 years	School nurse administered questionnaire to mothers about the child's health, development and use of services and parental health. Tests of ability and attainment administered at school.
1955	9 years	School nurse administered questionnaire to mothers about the child's health, development and use of services and parental health.
1956	10 years	Questionnaire sent to teachers about school type, amenities, child's progress and parental interest.

130

1957	11 years	Questionnaire sent to teachers about school type, amenities, child's progress and parental interest.
		Medical examination by school doctor.
		School nurse administered questionnaire to mothers about the child's health, development and use of services and parental health.
		Tests of ability and attainment administered at school.
1959	13 years	Questionnaire sent to teachers about school type, amenities, child's progress and parental interest, and teachers assessed child's behaviour.
		Survey members completed the Pintner Personality Inventory.
1960-61	14-15 years	Medical examination by school doctor.
1961	15 years	Questionnaire sent to teachers about school type, amenities, child's progress and parental interest, and teachers assessed child's behaviour.
		Questionnaire to head teachers about school circumstances and vocational guidance. Survey members completed a questionnaire about career aspirations and intentions.
		School nurse administered questionnaire to mothers about the child's health and use of services, employment aspirations and prospects and parental health, and mothers answered the short Maudsley Personality Inventory.
		Medical examination by school doctor.
		Tests of ability and attainment administered at school.

All hospital admissions were also checked with the hospitals concerned.

OFFENCES USED IN THE CONSTRUCTION OF THE
SOCIAL ACCEPTABILITY OF CRIME SCALE ARRANGED BY
SCORE VALUE

Score 1   No rear light on bicycle
Obstructing highway
Drunk and disorderly
Speeding
Not giving way at a pedestrian crossing
Unauthorised passenger on scooter with 'L' driver
Buying liquor under age
Disorderly behaviour
No motor vehicle licence

Trespass
Failure to conform to traffic sign
Purchasing ammunition
No bicycle brakes
Letting off fireworks in the street or public building
Breach of the peace
Committing a nuisance
False fire alarm
No gun licence

Score 2   Larceny
Receiving
Embezzlement
Driving without due care and attention
Careless driving
Unfit to drive through drink or drugs
Taking motor vehicle without the driver's consent
Shoplifting
Larceny by servant
Wilful damage
Frequenting
Driving while disqualified/uninsured
Loitering with intent
Aiding and abetting unauthorised taking of motor vehicle
Avoiding payment of a rail fare
Obtaining money by false pretences
Sacrilege
Unauthorised taking of a motor vehicle
Possessing an offensive weapon
Possessing house breaking tools

Score 3   Larceny from a vehicle
Taking a vehicle and theft of vehicle
Breaking and entering
Felony
Larceny from automatic machines
Malicious damage
Attempted break-in
House/shop/factory, etc. break-in

Score 4   Assault and actual bodily harm
Assault with intent to rob
Indecent assault
Bestiality
Rape
Malicious wounding

Unclassified   Indecent exposure
Inciting children to commit acts of indecency
Death by dangerous driving
Unlawful sexual intercourse with a female aged 13-16 years

SOCIAL-GROUP CLASSIFICATION IN THE NATIONAL SURVEY

The classification is based, for the most part, on the 1957 occupation of the father of the Survey child; where this is not known, it is based on the 1946 occupation.

Upper-middle class

The father is a non-manual worker, and
  (a) both parents went to secondary school and were brought up in middle-class families, or
  (b) both parents went to secondary school and one parent was brought up in a middle-class family, or
  (c) both parents were brought up in middle-class families and one parent went to secondary school.

Lower-middle class

The rest of the non-manual workers' families.

Upper-manual working class

The father is a manual worker and
  either the father or the mother or both of them had a secondary school education, and/or one or both of them were brought up in a middle-class family.

Lower-manual working class

The father is a manual worker, and
  both the father and the mother had elementary schooling only, and both the father and the mother were brought up in manual-working-class families.

Tests of Ability used at ages 8, 11 and 15 Years

The four tests given at age 8 were:

1. A 60-item non-verbal picture test.   Published by the NFER as Picture Test 1 by J. E. Stuart.

2. A 35-item reading comprehension test. Published by the NFER as Sentence Reading Test 1 by A. F. Watts.

3. A 50-item word reading test.   The same list of words was used in both these tests, which were also given at age

4. A 50-item vocabulary test.   11 years.

The four tests given at age 11 were:

1. An 80-item verbal and non-verbal ability test.   Alternate items verbal and non-verbal

2. A 50-item arithmetic test.   20 mechanical sums and 30 problems.

3. A 50-item mechanical word reading test. The same test given in the Survey at age 8 years.

4. A 50-item vocabulary test.   The same test given in the Survey
                                           at age 8 years.

The three tests given at age 15 were:
1. A 65-item verbal and non-verbal ability AH4 Group Ability test by A. W. Heim.
   test.

2. A 35-item test of reading   The Watts-Vernon Reading test.
   comprehension.

3. A 47-item mathematics test.   Constructed for the National Survey by
                                         the NFER.

Teachers' Assessments of Survey children's
Attitudes to work at age 10 Years (Four-Point Scale)
This question is one of eight about school achievement and behaviour.

Is this child in general:
  A very hard worker
  A hard worker
  An average worker
  A poor worker
  Lazy

Teachers' Assessments of Survey children at ages 15 and 13 Years

Child's attitude to school work

Which statement in each group *best* describes this child?
  A very hard worker
  Average — works moderately well
  A poor worker or lazy

  One with high power of concentration
  Average — concentrates moderately well
  Little or no power of sustained concentration

Extremely neat and tidy in class work   Seldom or never disobedient
Average — moderately neat and tidy   Sometimes disobedient
Very untidy in class work   Frequently disobedient

Seldom or never difficult to discipline   Seldom or never restless in class
Sometimes difficult to discipline   Sometimes restless in class
Frequently difficult to discipline   Frequently restless in class

Seldom or never daydreams in class   Seldom or never cribs
Sometimes daydreams in class   Sometimes cribs
Frequently daydreams in class   Frequently cribs

Seldom or never evades the truth to keep out of trouble
Sometimes evades the truth to keep out of trouble
Frequently evades the truth to keep out of trouble

*Has this child the ability to benefit from attending a University or Technical College for whole-time study?
　Yes, University
　Yes, Technical College
　Neither

Behaviour

Which statement in each group *best* describes this child?
　Liable to get unduly rough during playtime
　Takes a normal part in rough games
　Rather frightened of rough games

　Avoids attention, hates being in the limelight
　Does not unduly avoid or seek attention
　Shows off; seeks attention

　A dare-devil
　As cautious as the average child
　Extremely fearful

　Over-competitive with other children
　Normally competitive
　Diffident about competing with other children

　Unusually happy and contented child
　Generally cheerful and in good humour
　Usually gloomy and sad

　A quarrelsome and aggressive child
　Average — not particularly quarrelsome
　A timid child

　Makes friends extremely easily
　Takes usual amount of time to make friends
　Does not seem able to make friends

　*Extremely energetic, never tired
　Normally energetic
　Always tired and 'washed out'
　Not at all anxious, apprehensive or fearful
　Somewhat anxious, apprehensive or fearful
　Very anxious, apprehensive or fearful

How does this child react to criticism or punishment?
　Tends to become unduly resentful
　Tends to become unduly miserable or worried
　Normal attitude to criticism and punishment

Taking this child's behaviour and relationship with other children as a whole, would
you say he/she is —
    Sensitive or highly strung
    Shy or withdrawn
    Aggressive
    Other, namely

How well do you know this child?
    Very well
    Moderately well
    Not very well

*Not asked at 13 years

Doctors' Assessments of Physical Maturity

Boys

Assessments are based on the following questions in the school doctors' examination
forms, completed when the boys were 15:

Is any pigmented hair visible?	Yes, sparse
	Yes, profuse
	No
Is any axillary hair visible?	Yes
	No
Has the child's voice broken?	Not yet broken
	Starting to break
	Completely broken
Development of genitalia	Infantile
	Early*
	Advanced or complete**

The four maturity groups are:
(a) Mature — fully broken voice, axillary hair, profuse pubic hair, mature genitals;
(b) Advanced signs — genitals assessed as mature but one of the other maturity
            signs absent;
(c) Early signs — intermediate between advanced and infantile;
(d) Infantile — infantile genitals, no pubic or axillary hair, voice unbroken.

*Early: Increase in length of penis and width of glans with softening and slight
enlargement of testes.
**Advanced: Substantial enlargement of glans and penis plus testicular enlargement
with pendulous and rugose scrotum.

Girls

The girls are grouped by the age at which they had their first period (age of menarche):
(a) Very early menarche (before eleven years ten months);
(b) Early menarche (eleven years ten months and before twelve years ten months);
(c) Late menarche (twelve years ten months and before thirteen years ten months);
(d) Very late menarche (thirteen years ten months or later).

Bibliography

ADLER, A. (1932) *What Life Should Mean to You* London, Allen & Unwin.
ARCTANDER, S. (1936) in Otterstrom, E. (1946) 'Delinquency and children from bad homes' *Acta Paediatrica*, 33 Suppl. 5

BALDWIN, J. and BOTTOMS, A.E. (1976) *The Urban Criminal* London, Tavistock.
BANKS, C., MALONEY, E. and WILLCOCK, H.D. (1975) 'Public attitudes to crime and the penal system' *British Journal of Criminology* 15, p. 228
BECKER, H.S. (1963) *Outsiders* New York, Free Press.
BECKER, H.S. (1964) *Delinquency and Drift* New York, John Wiley
BELSON, W.A. (1968) 'The extent of stealing by London boys and some of its origins' *Advancement of Science* 25 p. 171
BERNSTEIN, B. (1973) *Class, Codes and Control* St. Albans, Paladin
BLACK, D.J. and REISS, A.J. (1970) 'Police control of juveniles' *American Sociological Review* 35, p. 63
BORRELL, B. and CASHINELLA, B. (1975) *Crime in Britain Today* London, Routledge & Kegan Paul
BOWLBY, J. (1947) *Forty Four Juvenile Thieves* London, Balliere, Tindall & Cox
BOWLBY, J., AINSWORTH, M., BOSTON, M. and ROSENBLUTH, D. (1956) 'The effects of mother-child separation: a follow-up study' *British Journal of Medical Psychology* 29, p. 211
BOWLBY, J. and PARKES, C.D. (1970) *Separation and Loss within the Family* in E.J. Anthony and C.M. Koupernik (eds) *The Child in his Family* Chichester, John Wiley
BOX, S. (1971) *Deviance, Reality & Society* London, Holt Rinehart & Winston
BURT, C. (1925) *The Young Delinquent* University of London Press, fourth, revised edition, 1944
BUTLER, N.R., DOWLING, S. and OSBOURN, S. *Child Health and Education in the Seventies* Department of Child Health, University of Bristol

CARTWRIGHT, A. (1963) 'Memory errors in a morbidity survey' *Milbank Memorial Fund Quarterly* 61, p. 1
CENTRAL STATISTICAL OFFICE (1975) *Social Trends* London, HMSO

CLARK, J.P. and WENNINGER, E.P. (1962) 'Socio economic class and area as correlates of illegal behaviour among juveniles' *American Sociological Review* 27, p. 826

CLARKE, A.M. and CLARKE,. A.D.B. (1976) *Early Experience: Myth and Evidence* London, Open Books

COCHRANE, R. (1974) 'Crime and personality: theory and evidence' *Bulletin of the British Psychological Society* 27, p. 19

CORTES, J.B. and GATTI, F.M. (1972) *Delinquency and Crime: a Biopsychosocial Approach* New York, Seminar Press

COWIE, J., COWIE, V. and SLATER, E. (1968) *Delinquency in Girls* London, Heinemann

Criminal Statistics (England and Wales) (1973, 1974, 1975 and 1976) Cmnd. 5677, 6168, 6566 and 6909, HMSO

DALTON, K. (1961) 'Menstruation and crime' *British Medical Journal* 2, p. 1752

DAVIE, R., BUTLER, N.R. and GOLDSTEIN, H. (1972) *From Birth to Seven* London, Longman

DAVIES, J.G.V. and MALIPHANT, R. (1974) 'Refractory behaviour in school and avoidance learning' *Journal of Child Psychology and Psychiatry* 15, p. 23

DOUGLAS, J.W.B. (1964) *The Home and the School* London, McGibbon & Kee

DOUGLAS, J.W.B. (1975) 'Early hospital admissions and later disturbances of behaviour and learning' *Developmental Medicine and Child Neurology* 17, p. 456

DOUGLAS, J.W.B. and BLOMFIELD, J.M. (1956) 'The reliability of longitudinal surveys' *Milbank Memorial Fund Quarterly* 34, p. 228

DOUGLAS, J.W.B. and BLOMFIELD, J.M. (1958) *Children Under Five* London, Allen & Unwin

DOUGLAS, J.W.B. and ROSS, J.M. (1964) 'Age of puberty related to educational ability, attainment and school leaving age' *Journal of Child Psychology & Psychiatry* 5, p. 185

DOUGLAS, J.W.B., ROSS, J.M. and SIMPSON, H.R. (1968) *All our Future* London, Peter Davies

DOUGLAS, J.W.B., ROSS, J.M., HAMMOND, W.A. and MULLIGAN, D.G. (1966) 'Delinquency and social class' *British Journal of Criminology* 6, p. 294

DOUGLAS, J.W.B. and SIMPSON, H.R. (1964) 'Height in relation to puberty, family size and social class' *Milbank Memorial Fund Quarterly* 42, p. 20

ERIKSON, K.T. (1962) 'Notes on the Sociology of Deviance' *Social Problems* 9, p. 308

EYSENCK, H.J. (1958) 'A short questionnaire for the measurement of two dimensions of personality' *Journal of Applied Psychology* 43, p. 14

EYSENCK, H.J. (1964) *Crime and Personality* London, Routledge & Kegan Paul

EYSENCK, S.B.G. and EYSENCK, H.J. (1970) 'Crime and personality: an empirical study of the three-factor theory' *British Journal of Criminology* 10, p. 225

FERGUSON, T. (1952) *The Young Delinquent in his Social Setting* London, Oxford University Press

FORTES, M. (1933) 'The influence of position in sibships on juvenile delinquency' *Econometrica* 13, p. 301

FUCHS-KAMP, A. (1929) in Otterstrom, E. (1946) 'Delinquency and children from bad homes' *Acta Paediatrica*, 33 Suppl. 5

GATH, D., TENNENT, G. and PIDDUCK, R. (1970) 'Educational characteristics of bright delinquents' *British Journal of Educational Psychology* 40, p. 216

GIBBENS, T.C.N. (1963) *Psychiatric Studies of Borstal Lads* Oxford University Press

GIBBENS, T.C.N. and PRINCE, J. (1962) *Shoplifting* London, Institute for the Study and Treatment of Delinquency

GLASS, D.V. (ed.) (1954) *Social Mobility in Great Britain* London, Routledge & Kegan Paul

GLUECK, S. and GLUECK, E. (1940) *Juvenile Delinquents Grown Up* New York, The Commonwealth Fund

GLUECK, S. and GLUECK, E. (1950) *Unravelling Juvenile Delinquency,* Cambridge, Mass., Harvard University Press

GLUECK, S. and GLUECK, E. (1956) *Physique and Delinquency* New York, Harper & Row

GOLDSTEIN, H. (1969) 'Longitudinal studies and the measurement of change' *The Statistician* 18, p. 93

GORING, C. (1919) *The English Convict,* abridged edition with an introduction by K. Pearson, London, HMSO

GRAY, P.G. (1955) 'The memory factor in social surveys' *Journal of the American Statistical Association* 50, p. 344

HADDON, W., SUCHMAN, E.A. and KLEIN, D. (1964) *Accident Research* New York, Harper & Row

HARGREAVES, D.H. (1967) *Social Relations in a Secondary School* London, Routledge & Kegan Paul

HOOD, R. and SPARKS, R. (1970) *Key Issues in Criminology* London, Weidenfeld & Nicolson

ILLSLEY, R. and THOMPSON, J. (1961) 'Women from broken homes' *Sociological Review* 9, p. 27

JACKSON, B. and MARSDEN, D. (1962) *Education and the Working Class* London, Routledge & Kegan Paul

KAGAN, J. (1976) 'Resilience and Continuity in Psychological Development' in A.M. Clarke and A.D.B. Clarke *Early Experience: Myth and Evidence* London, Open Books

KAYSER, B.D. (1974) 'Response bias in children's reports of parental status characteristics' *Social Focus* 7, p. 61

LEWIS, H. (1954) *Deprived Children* Oxford University Press

LIEDERMAN, P.H. and SHAPIRO, D. (eds) (1964) *Psychobiological Approaches to Social Behaviour* Stanford University Press

LIPPMAN, W. (1922) *Public Opinion* New York, Macmillan

LOMBROSO, C. and FERRERO, W. (1895) *The Female Offender* London, Fisher Unwin

LOMBROSO, C. (1913) *Crime: Its Causes and Remedies* Boston, Little, Brown

McCORD, W., McCORD, J. and ZOLA, I.K. (1959) *Origins of Crime* Columbia University Press

McCORD, W. and McCORD, J. (1964) *The Psychopath* Princeton, N.J., Van Nostrand

McDONALD, L. (1969) *Social Class and Delinquency* London, Faber & Faber

McCLINTOCK, F.H. (1963) *Crimes of Violence* London, Macmillan

McCLINTOCK, F.H. and AVISON, N.H. (1968) *Crime in England and Wales* London, Routledge & Kegan Paul

MANNHEIM, H. (1965) *Comparative Criminology* London, Routledge & Kegan Paul

MARCUS, B. (1956) 'Intelligence, criminality and the expectation of recidivism' *British Journal of Delinquency* 6, p. 147

MARRIS, P. (1958) *Widows and their Families* London, Routledge & Kegan Paul

MARTIN, J.P. (1962) *Offenders as Employees* London, Macmillan

MARTIN, J.P. and WILSON, G. (1969) *The Police: A Study in Manpower* London, Heinemann

MATZA, D. (1964) *Delinquency and Drift* Chichester, John Wiley

MATZA, D. (1969) *Becoming Deviant* New York, Prentice-Hall

MAYER, R. (1946) *Young People in Trouble* London, Gollancz

MAYHEW, P., CLARKE, R.V.G., STURMAN, A. and HOUGH, J.M. (1976) *Crime as Opportunity* Home Office Research Studies No. 34, London, HMSO

MERTON, R.K. (1957) *Social Theory & Social Structure* New York, Free Press

MILLER, D.R. and SWANSON, G.E. (1958) *The Changing American Parent* New York, John Wiley

MILLER, E. (1944) 'The Problem of Birth Order and Delinquency' in L. Radzinowicz and J.W.C. Turner *Mental Abnormality and Crime* London, Macmillan, English Studies in Criminal Science, vol. 2

MORRIS, D.P., SOROKER, E. and BURRUSS, G. (1954) 'Follow-up studies of shy withdrawn children — evaluation of later adjustment' *American Journal of Orthopsychiatry* 24, p. 743

MORRIS, T.P. (1957) *The Criminal Area* London, Routledge & Kegan Paul

MULLIGAN, D.G. (1964) 'Some correlates of maladjustment in a national sample of school-children' unpublished PhD. thesis, University of London

MURPHY, F.J., SHIRLEY, M.M. and WITMER, H.L. (1946) 'The incidence of hidden delinquency' *American Journal of Orthopsychiatry* 16, p. 686

NETTLER, G. (1974) *Explaining Crime* London, McGraw Hill

NEWMAN, O. (1972) *Defensible Space* London, Architectural Press

NEWSON, J. and NEWSON, E. (1968) *Four Years Old in an Urban Community* London, Allen & Unwin

NISSELSON, H. and WOOLSEY, T.D. (1959) 'Some problems of the household interview design for the National Health Survey' *Journal of the American Statistical Association* 54, p. 69

NYE, F.I. (1958) *Family Relations and Delinquent Behaviour* New York, John Wiley

OTTERSTROM, E. (1946) 'Delinquency and Children from Bad Homes' *Acta Paediatrica*, 33 Suppl. 5

PILIAVIN, I. and BRIAR, S. (1964) 'Police encounters with juveniles' *American Journal of Sociology* 70, p. 206

PINTNER, R. (1938) 'Four tests of a personality inventory' *Journal of Educational Psychology* 29, p. 93

PLESS, I.B. and DOUGLAS, J.W.B. (1971) 'Chronic illness in childhood' *Paediatrics* 47, p. 405

POLLACK, O. (1961) *The Criminality of Women* New York, Barnes

POWERS, E. and WITMER, H. (1951) *An Experiment in the Prevention of Delinquency: the Cambridge-Somerville Youth Study* New York, Columbia University Press

RAAB, W.C. (1971) 'Cardiotoxic biochemical effects of emotional-environmental stresses', in L. Levi (ed.) *Society, Stress and Disease* Oxford University Press

RADZINOWICZ, L. and KING, J. (1977) *The Growth of Crime* London, Hamish Hamilton

ROBERTSON, J. and BOWLBY, J. (1952) 'Responses of young children to separation from their mothers' *Courr. Centr. Int. L'Enfance* 2, p. 131

ROBINS, L.N. (1966) *Deviant Children Grown up* Baltimore, Williams & Wilins

ROFF, M. (1961) 'Childhood social interaction and young adult bad conduct' *Journal of Abnormal Social Psychology* 63, p. 333

ROSS, J.M. and SIMPSON, H.R. (1971a) 'The National Survey of Health and Development: Part I Educational attainment' *British Journal of Educational Psychology* 41, p. 49

Ross, J.M. and Simpson, H.R. (1971b) 'The rate of school progress between 8 and 15 years and between 15 and 18 years' *British Journal of Educational Psychology* 41, p. 125

Rossi, P.H., Waite, E., Bose, C.E. and Berk, R.E. (1974) 'The seriousness of crime' *American Sociological Review* 39, p. 224

Rutter, M. (1966) *Children of Sick Parents* Oxford University Press

Scheff, T. (1966) *Being Mentally Ill: A Sociological Theory* Chicago, Aldine Press

Schofield, M. (1968) *The Sexual Behaviour of Young People* London, Penguin

Schur, E.M. (1971) *Labelling Deviant Behaviour* New York, Harper & Row

Schur, E.M. (1973) *Radical Non-Intervention* New York, Prentice-Hall

Sears, R.R., Maccoby, E.E. and Levin, H. (1957) *Patterns of Child Rearing* New York, Row Peterson

Sellin, T. and Wolfgang, M.E. (1964) *The Measurement of Delinquency* London, John Wiley

Shaw, C.R. and McKay, H. (1931) *Social Factors in Juvenile Delinquency* Washington, U.S. Government Printing Office

Sheldon, W.H. (1949) *Varieties of Delinquent Youth* New York, Harper & Row

Simcha-Fagan, O., Langner, T.S., Gersten, J.C. and Eisenberg, J.G. (mimeo) 'Violent and antisocial behaviour: interim report of a longitudinal study of urban youth' New York, Columbia University, School of Public Health, Family Research Project

Simmons, J.L. (1969) *Deviants* Berkeley, Glendessary Press

Smart, C. (1976) *Women, Crime and Criminology* London, Routledge & Kegan Paul

Smith, S.L. (1975) 'Female delinquency and social reaction' mimeo

Sparks, R.F., Genn, H.G. and Dodd, D.J. (1977) *Surveying Victims* Chichester, John Wiley

Spitz, R.A. and Wolf, K. (1946) 'Anaclitic depression' *Journal for the Psychoanalytic Study of the Child* 2, p. 313

Sterne, R.S. (1964) *Delinquent Conduct and Broken Homes* Connecticut, College and University Press

Stott, D.H. (1950) *Delinquency and Human Nature* Scotland, Carnegie Trust

Tanner, J.M. (1962) *Growth at Adolescence* Oxford, Blackwell

Taylor, I., Walton, P. and Young, J. (1973) *The New Criminology* London, Routledge & Kegan Paul

Thomas, W.I. (1907) *Sex and Society* Boston, Little Brown

Tong, J.E. and Murphy, I.C. (1960) 'A review of stress reactivity research in relation to psychopathology and psychopathic behaviour disorders' *Journal of Mental Science* 106, p. 1273

Turk, A. (1969) *Criminality and the Legal Order* Chicago, Rand McNally

WADSWORTH, M.E.J. (1975) 'Delinquency in a national sample of children' *British Journal of Criminology* 15, p. 167

WADSWORTH, M.E.J. (1976) 'Delinquency, pulse rates and early emotional deprivation' *British Journal of Criminology* 16, p. 265

WADSWORTH, M.E.J. (1978) 'Delinquency prediction and its uses: the experience of a twenty one year follow-up study' *International Journal of Mental Health,* 7

WADSWORTH, M.E.J. (in preparation) 'The social context and its effect on research'

WALKER, M.A. (1979) 'Measuring the seriousness of crimes' *British Journal of Criminology,* in press

WALKER, N. (1965) *Crime and Punishment in Britain* Edinburgh University Press

WALKER, N. (1971) *Crimes, Courts and Figures* Harmondsworth, Penguin

WALL, W.D. (1968) *Adolescents in School and Society* Slough, National Foundation for Educational Research

WALLERSTEIN, J.S. and WYLE, C.L. (1947) 'Our lawabiding lawbreakers' *National Probation,* March, p. 107

WATSON, J.D. (1950) *The Child and the Magistrate* London, Jonathan Cape

WATTENBERG, W.W. and SAUNDERS, F. (1954) 'Sex differences among juvenile offenders' *Sociology and Social Research* 39, p. 24

WEEKS, A. (1940) 'Male and female broken home rate by type of delinquency' *American Sociological Review* 5, p. 601

WEST, D.J. (1967) *The Young Offender* London, Duckworth

WEST, D.J. (1969) *Present Conduct and Future Delinquency* London, Heinemann

WEST, D.J. and FARRINGTON, D.P. (1973) *Who Becomes Delinquent?* London, Heinemann

WEST, D.J. and FARRINGTON, D.P. (1977) *The Delinquent Way of Life* London, Heinemann

WOLFF, S. (1969) *Children Under Stress* London, Allen Lane

WOOTTON, B. (1959) *Social Science and Social Pathology* London, George Allen & Unwin

WORLD HEALTH ORGANISATION (1951) *Expert Committee on Mental Health: Report on the Second Session* Geneva

YARROW, L.J. (1961) 'Maternal deprivation: toward an empirical and conceptual re-evaluation' *Psychological Bulletin* 58, p. 459

YARROW, M.R., CAMPBELL, J.D. and BURTON, R.V. (1970) *Recollections of Childhood: A Study of the Retrospective Method* Monograph of the Society for Research in Child Development No. 138

Author Index

Subject Index